the HOW TO WRITE A BOOK *book*

the HOW TO WRITE A BOOK *book*

Robert F. Mager

The Center for Effective Performance, Inc., Atlanta, Georgia

Other Books by Robert F. Mager

Analyzing Performance Problems. 2nd ed., 1984. (with Peter Pipe)
Developing Attitude Toward Learning. 2nd ed., 1984.
Goal Analysis. 2nd ed., 1984.
Making Instruction Work. 1988.
Measuring Instructional Results. 2nd ed., 1984.
Preparing Instructional Objectives. 2nd ed., 1984.
Troubleshooting the Troubleshooting Course. 2nd ed., 1984.

Permissions:

Peanuts by Charles Schultz © by and permission from United Features Syndicate.
B.C. by Johnny Hart © by and permission from News America Syndicate.
Family Circus by Bill Keane © by and permission from Cowles Syndicate.
Marvin by Tom Armstrong © by and permission from News America Syndicate.

ISBN-1-8796-1800-1

Library of Congress Catalog number: 85-090492

Printed in the United States of America

1.987654321

Contents

A Magerfable

Once upon a time, in a meadow close to home, Hapily Porcupine decided to write a book. "Yes," he mused, the exciting thought dancing through his brain, "I'll call it Loveneedles.*"*

"Ooch, eech, ouch," he said, as he yanked a quill from his hide and set to work. It was very slow going, especially since his quills wore out and his skin began to show. And even more especially because his mind was new to this kind of think-do. Even so, he was determined to finish what he started.

One day, Upity Ostrich loped by and said, "What in the world are you doing?"

"I'm writing a book," replied Hapily, happily. "Aren't you?"

"Are you mad*?" shrieked Upity, uppily. "I don't have the* time *for that sort of thing; and besides, I'm sure it's much too* hard*," and went on her way. And Hapily went back to work.*

Not long afterward he heard a slithering in the bush.

"Sssssssaay," said Snerfy the Snake, "what are you doing?"

"I'm writing a book," replied Hapily, happily. "Aren't you?"

"Aw, gee, n-no," mumbled Snerfy, sniffily. "Just look at me. Who am I to be writing a book about anything? I don't even have anything to write with. You, on the other . . . er . . . hand—why, you're positively bristling with writing equipment," and slithered on his way. And Hapily went back to work.

One day he heard a flapping in the air, after which Hawtily Hawk plopped onto a branch.

"And just what do you think you're *doing?" asked Hawtily, haughtily.*

"I'm writing a book," replied Hapily, happily. "Aren't you?"

"Certainly not*" replied Hawtily, preening a wing with her beak. "I couldn't possibly do a thing like* that, *dear boy. Besides, what would people* say? *I'm sure it would be* most *embarrassing," whereupon she swooped away. And Hapily went back to work.*

One day, when the wind was still and the sun was warm, Hapily chanced upon his friends, tsking in the meadow.

"Hello, good friends," said Hapily, happily. "What are you doing?"

"Why, we're reviewing *this book you call* Loveneedles,*" they clucked.*

*"*I *would have made it longer," said one.*

*"*I *would have made it shorter," said another.*

*"*I *would have made it better," snided the third.*

"Oh, I expect you're all very *correct," said Hapily, sincerely. Whereupon he began to smile. And the smile turned into a giggle, and the giggle turned into the biggest bellylaugh that Hapily had ever owned. Because unlike his friends, Hapily had just learned the secret of life: Persistence makes accomplishments; excuses make hot air.*

And so the moral of this fable is

If you're sure you can't, you won't.
If you think you can, you might.
If you know you can, you will.

And indeed he was right. False perceptions about our own abilities often keep us from succeeding, or even attempting to succeed, in areas we just "know" are beyond us—such as writing. Many people want to write a book, but hold back because, well . . . because of any number of reasons. If *you* have collected one or more "reasons" for not writing the book you have wanted to write, or need to write, or know you *should* write, read on. Though the pages that follow won't teach you the mechanics of writing, they will show you how to skewer the excuses, leap 'round the obstacles, and find joy in the very act of writing. And then you, too, will be able to say, happily, "I wrote a book."

R.F. Mager
Carefree, Arizona

Why?

You sit there with a blank piece of paper, ready to start your book. Your pencil is poised, or your fingers hover expectantly over the keyboard.

Now what? Where do you begin? What do you do next? How do you know when you're done? And then what?

If you are starting your first book, you will face these and similar questions time and time again. You will wonder what to do next; you will wonder if it is worth continuing; and you will find excuses to quit. You will wish you knew the secrets of how to make the muse strike and how to keep yourself at it until it is finished and ready to go to press.

As you have suspected, successful writing involves more than just putting words on paper. It involves knowing how to get yourself started, how to keep yourself going, and how to know when you're done. Perhaps more important, it involves knowing how to avoid the traps that would cause you to stop dead in your tracks and quit before you're finished.

And *that* is something I can help you with. Not with how to *write,* but with how to *write a book*. I can show you how to begin, how to keep yourself from quitting, and how to handle the major writing traps. I can offer you a procedure for shaping your book into one that has the effect you want it to have on your readers. And I can show you how to withstand the slings and arrows of those who would shoot you down before you start— or before you finish. That's a lot. It isn't everything, but it's a lot. And it's the key to successful writing, because if you don't get it *down*, you can't get it *good*.

Why do I feel qualified to write a book about writing a book? Because I'm just like you. I'm not a professional writer, and I don't write for a living. I wrote only one paragraph in my entire life that an English teacher ever said anything nice about. I don't know a noun clause from an adjective phrase, and I'm the kind of guy who thinks an ablative is something you take for constipation.

Even so, I've managed to write seven books (five solo and two with co-authors). All have been published, more than 2,000,000 copies have been sold, and, as of this writing, all are still in print.

I find sitting down with that blank piece of paper as onerous as you do (or will), and I've invented all sorts of ways to avoid it. But I've also found some ways to get on with it. I've found some ploys to make it easier, some to make the writing itself more enjoyable, and some to help make sure the finished book works.

So, if you're thinking about writing a book, I think I can be of help.

Everybody Writes

Everybody writes!

It's true. Everybody writes letters, shopping lists, memos, reports, love notes, foot notes, or themes. Some write lab notes, engineering reports, or dissertations. Others write proposals, personnel evaluations, case summaries, or crime reports.

Everybody writes, but not all people think of themselves as being "Writers." Why do you suppose that is? Is it because they have never earned money or made a living from writing? Nooo, it can't be that, because there are any number of people who *call* themselves writers who have never had a word of theirs published.

Then what's the difference between someone who writes and a "Writer"? Is it that a "real" writer writes good stuff and others don't? That can't be it, either. If you think back over all the junk you've read, you'll realize that quality can't be the difference.

Then what? Is it that "real" writers have a magic touch or native ability that allows them to sit down and immediately turn on the flow of sparkling words from their fingers? No. If that was it there wouldn't be so many successful writers who have written about the pain, the anguish, the tedium of writing.

If a "real" writer isn't someone who makes more money at writing than you do, or necessarily someone who writes better than you do, or who writes faster or more easily than you do, then what's the difference between us and them? State of mind, that's what. The difference is that we don't *think* of ourselves as writers. I've written several books and, even though they have been published, I don't *think* of myself as a Real Writer; if you haven't written your first book you probably don't, either.

Worse, you may think that "real" writers are somehow so different from you that it would take buckets of talent and years of training to be like them. That's hogwash (and an obstacle to writing). Some writers have a real talent for it, of course, but many write without it. Some writers write rapidly, and others are as slow as molasses. But none of them are so different from you that you can't write something worth reading. All you need is to get started, and to stick with it until it's done.

And that's where I think I can help. I can show you how to get yourself started, how to keep yourself going, how to make sure your book does what you want it to do, and how to know when you're done. I'll even offer a few tips on how to get it published.

What I *won't* do is to tell you how to write sentences, or how to plot stories, or how to spell. This isn't a book on how to write, after all; it's about how to *write a book.* Besides, there's plenty of help available on the mechanics of writing. But I will show you how to get others to help in checking and improving your content, your sequence, and your use of words—all for free. Just remember this:

What you write may be good, or it may not be.
But if it isn't written, *it isn't* anything.
So let's get started.

What's a Book?

What's a book? That may seem like a strange question. After all, everyone knows what a book is, right? Wrong. And unless your perception of a book is in proper focus you will face yet another obstacle to success.

The first "book" I ever had published (the one that has sold more than 2,000,000 copies during the past twenty-two years) was only sixty-two pages long. Sixty-two pages? And you call that a *book*? Worse, the text was only on the right-hand pages. Oh, there was a paragraph or two in italics on a few of the left-hand pages (called *verso* in the book biz), but it was still only sixty-two pages long.

Shortly after the book was published, a professor who reviewed it suggested that it was far too short to be called a book; he suggested that it was more of a pamphlet. Maybe he was right. But so what? Where is it written that a book is a stuffy tome of more than 500 pages? Or 300 pages? Or even 100 pages? What does it matter how long it is as long as it serves a purpose? One of my colleagues wrote a little book on how to classify trees in Great Britain. Talk about small. The pages were only about four inches on a side, and there were only thirty-two of them. But it turned out to be extremely useful to a lot of people. It's small, it serves a purpose, and many people have bought it. What more would you want?

So a book is what you make it, or what you call it. If it feels good to call your work a book, do it. If it feels good to call it something else, do that. Just get it written, no matter how long or short it turns out to be.

The point is worth picking at. (Notice how that sentence ends in a preposition? And you thought they weren't something you could end a sentence with.) *[I'll let that pass. Ed.]* When you sit down to write your book your first thought should be on making it do what you want it to do. You should *not* think about how long it will be, or whether you will have enough pages to make it worth publishing. If it serves a purpose, it's worth publishing, and someone will publish it. There are thousands of works that have been worth publishing that are only *one* page long. There are charts, graphs, posters, job aids, checklists, poems, fables, and many others. You might not call them books, but so what? It isn't the *length* that gives it value; it's the substance. If it's useful (whether for informing or entertaining), it's worth creating—regardless of its length.

Firming the Resolve

"People don't do things for the darnedest reasons," said a colleague of mine while recounting his experience with golf. He'd wanted to be a golfer for a long time. He finally bought some clubs and signed up for a college course on "Beginning Golf." Though he completed the course, it was two years before he actually played on a golf course. What took him so long? Why the procrastination? Let him tell it.

"Well, I wanted to, but something kept holding me back. It wasn't until some months later that I realized my reluctance was caused by a lack of knowledge. Though my golf course had taught me the rudiments of the game, it didn't teach me how to get onto a golf course—and I was embarrassed to ask someone. I didn't have any idea of what the procedure was for getting onto a course, and I had images of myself being humiliated because of my 'stupidity.'"

He was right. People don't do things for the darnedest reasons.

So what's your excuse—excuse me—*reason*, for not writing that book you've been thinking about? Check one or more of the following.

______ I don't have anything "important" to say.
______ Maybe nobody would want to read it.
______ It's already been done.
______ I don't have the time.
______ I'm not creative.
______ What would people say?
______ Who am I to write about this subject?
______ I don't know how.
______ It would never be published.

If you're normal, you would check any or all of those items at one time or another, and maybe some I haven't listed. Maybe they're good reasons for not writing. And maybe they're not. Let's check them out.

I don't have anything "Important" to say

You don't say! What makes you think you have to have something important to say in order to write successfully? Do you think everyone has to be some sort of sage or prophet to write? There are all kinds of nonprophet writing. Haven't you ever read a story that delighted you? Or that amused you? Sure you have. Did the author have to have something to *say*? Did there have to be some sort of message or moral to make you feel your reading time was well spent? Hardly.

Have you ever played a musical instrument just for the fun of it? If so, you weren't necessarily "saying" something. Rather, you were expressing yourself, and perhaps sharing your experience and some joy with others. What about song writers? Sure, some of them write songs with messages. But not many, thank goodness. So if a song writer can write songs that please, or that serve a purpose, without having anything to "say," you can write for the same reasons.

Besides, not having something to say isn't at all the same as writing something not worth reading. Lots of people who have a great deal to say do a miserable job of saying it. And vice versa.

Thoughts about not having something to say can lead to quitting before you start, and need to be dealt with. So let's deal with them. When you think about it for a moment, you will see that the expression "something to say" is about as clear as IRS tax instructions. It is a murky expression that leads people into wrongthink, because it has too many possible meanings, none of which matter. That's right. The entire issue of having something to say is irrelevant to writing a book. It is a red herring, a false god, an empty idol. It isn't a matter of having "something to say"; it is a matter of having something to *share*.

Perhaps you know how to do something that you'd like to teach others, or perhaps you'd like to share an easier way of learning it. Perhaps you have a story to tell, or some chuckles to offer. Maybe you'd like to share some experiences, and maybe you'd like to put down what you know about a given subject. I'll bet you have "something to say" in at least one of these categories, and maybe in others I haven't mentioned. It might take as much work for you as it does for me to get it down, but I'll bet you have something worth sharing.

Maybe you write for professional journals and would like to write something for a broader audience. Maybe you lead a dull life and would like to tell the world about the boredom of it all. Or maybe you'd like to end that boredom by writing about some exciting adventures. Edgar Rice Burroughs did that to break up the boredom of bookkeeping. He created Tarzan. Maybe you are a student who feels the need to explain something more clearly. Whoever you are and whatever is pushing you inside, let it out. Give it a go. Even if nobody reads it, you will feel better for having written.

I remember the first two pieces I ever wrote. One was written to fill a need and the other was written in exasperation. When I finished basic training in the army I was assigned as a company clerk (because I could use two fingers on a typewriter). Recruits arrived in batches, still dazed from their sudden snatch from civilian life. They were ordered here and ordered there, and they tried as best they could to do what had to be done. But they were expected to do things they didn't know how to do and to do things they were never told about. I felt very, very sorry for those recruits and bitter toward those in charge who treated them like cattle. So I wrote a little manual to explain the simple rules by which the camp operated—a manual in which I tried to show the recruits the ropes. Then I went out and bought a mimeograph machine (which is now the only antique I own), typed the stencils, and went to press. I didn't ask permission to do it, and I didn't tell anybody what I was doing. It seemed like something that needed to be done, and so I did it.

And was it ever corny! I drew a cartoon for the cover (I am definitely *not* a cartoonist) and wrote in a balloon this gut-clutching poetry:

Start in now
Start right away
To be the best soldier
In Company "A"

Trite? Whooo-eee! And the innards weren't much better, considering the corny couplet I created for the bottom of each page.

But you know what? Copies were distributed to each incoming soldier on his arrival, and within a week all the other company commanders in the battalion wanted copies for *their* soldiers. So, while it wasn't much, it filled a need. Better than that, I was reimbursed for the money I spent, was called for an "audience" with the battalion commander, and became a medium-sized fish in a very small pond.

Did I have a "message"? No. I saw a need, and I went ahead and did my best to fill it. The fact that no "real" writer or critic would have had anything good to say about the prose was totally irrelevant. I wrote something that filled a need, and it was appreciated by those it was written for. Could I call it a book? Who cares!

The other piece was written a few years later while I was in graduate school. One day I was completely baffled and exasperated by my inability to understand one of the mathematical concepts being explained by the professor. So, just for my own private and personal satisfaction, I wrote out a step-by-step description of the concept, added an example or two at each point along the way to verify my understanding, and finished up with a short series of test items and explained answers. Naturally, I had to ask a lot of questions before I was finished, but by trying to write an instructional summary I knew which questions to ask. One day I showed it (about ten pages' worth) to somebody and was immediately engulfed with requests for copies. Years later I was astonished to learn that dittoed copies of that piece were given to all incoming graduate students for several years afterward (though they did remove my name from it).

Once again I didn't have anything to "say." I wrote something because *I* needed it, and then discovered that *others* found it useful as well.

So you don't have to have a message to have a reason to write, and not having anything to "say" is a poor excuse for not getting on with it. Besides, you may not be the best judge of what is worth writing. So go ahead and write it, whatever it is. You have nothing to lose and everything to gain.

Maybe nobody will want to read it

Maybe you're right. Maybe nobody *will* want to read it. Maybe people would laugh at it, or say nasty things about it. Maybe, maybe.

But wait a minute? Who are *you* to say whether or not anybody will want to read it? How can you tell if someone will want to read your stuff *before you even write it*? You can't! First say what you want to say, and then find out what you need to do to it so that other people *will* want to read it. (I'll show you how to do that in a later chapter.)

Can you imagine what we could have lost if Michelangelo had convinced himself that nobody would want to look at his painting? I can hear it now (with apologies to Michelangelo):

Sponsor	*Hey, Mike!*
Mich	*Yeah?*
Sponsor	*Why don'cha paint something for the Sistine Chapel?*
Mich	*Aw, I'm not good enough for that.*
Sponsor	*Sure you are. You could paint something terrific on the ceiling.*
Mich	*On the ceiling? Are you crazy?*
Sponsor	*No. It would look great!*
Mich	*You gotta be kidding.*
Sponsor	*It would dress the place up, give it some class.*
Mich	*On the ceiling? Nobody paints on ceilings.*
Sponsor	*So start a trend.*
Mich	*Who wants a stiff neck from looking at a ceiling? They'd be too far away to enjoy it. Maybe they wouldn't like it there. Besides, how would I get up there? How do I know I can paint lying on my back?*

It sounds a little silly when you hear *other* people quit before they start, when you hear *them* excuse themselves by pretending to read the minds of others. It should, because it is a poor excuse. It isn't an excuse used *only* by should-be writers, but it is a poor one nonetheless.

There may be any number of reasons why people might not want to read what you have written. It may be too long, or too boring. It could be on a subject people are tired of, or one they are too naive to understand. Then again, they may not want to read it because it was pompously written or because you wrote in governmentese. Oh, there are many reasons. But notice. They are reasons why someone may not want to read what you *have written*. They are *not* reasons for *not writing it*.

You can't win if you don't play.

Even if it isn't as successful as you hope, you will be immensely richer for having written it. You will have had practice (the next one will be better), and you will have in your hand

something that you created. There's a lot of satisfaction in that, published or not. Once in my life I created an oil painting. I've had no training in art, and I have no talent for it. But we were hobbying around one evening, and I was allowed to poke paint at one of my wife's canvasses. The result is more like a cartoon than a painting. The perspective is all wrong and the colors aren't right. But I *did* it. The painting (notice how I refer to it as "the painting") hangs in an obscure corner of a bathroom, and I don't care that it isn't good enough for a museum (it hangs in a loo instead of the Louvre). And people can be as critical of it as they want; that doesn't bother me. After all, it doesn't take skill to be critical. At least I provided them with something to be critical *of*.

So one more time. You can't find out whether anyone will want to read what you have written *until* you have written it.

It's already been done

Yes, it probably has. After all, there's nothing new under the sun, right? If you've seen one you've seen 'em all. You couldn't possibly write about anything that hasn't been written about before, could you? Or that is different from those that already exist. Look at all the books there are in the library, and on the bookstands. Thousands upon thousands. There couldn't be room for another one. Yes, it's all been done.

If you believe that, you'll believe anything. Can you imagine how many songs and operas and symphonies were written before a fellow named Gershwin appeared on the scene? Or the number of musical "sounds" that had been created before Glenn Miller came along? The number of mystery stories that had been written before Agatha Christie took a whack at it?

Over the years all sorts of comic strips have been created and populated with a brilliant variety of characters. Especially talking animals. A few years ago, though, a cartoonist came along and created still another dog. His name is Snoopy. Can you imagine the world of enjoyment that would have been lost if Charles Schultz had said, "Aw, it's already been done," and quit before he started?

You may not have the talent to become another Hemingway or Michener or Spillane. Neither do I. So what? That isn't important. What *is* important is that if you have something you want to write about you shouldn't let anything stand in your way—*least* of all a zany (and untrue) idea like "it's already been done." It's quite possible that you can make it better, more timely, more modern, or more something else. You just can't be sure that it's been done until you do it *your way.*

At the risk of beating this point into a blunt instrument, just take a closer look at that expression, "It's already been done." *What* has been done? The usual meaning of that expression is that something has been written on the topic or *subject* being considered. The implication is that the *subject* has been written about. But there are many sides to a subject, many emphases, many points of view. Even if there were only *one*, there are many ways in which it might be handled, some of which would be more useful or more appreciated than others.

One thing is clear. *Your* treatment of the subject has never been done. So it couldn't possibly have "been done"—unless you are the one who did it.

I don't have time to write

You've heard people say that. And if they say *that*, they also say they don't have time to read, or to play with their kids, or to take a course, or to communicate with their spouse.

Maybe they're right. After all, we all have only twenty-four hours in each day and we can't do everything. But hold on. Who said anything about doing everything? We're talking only about writing. Oh, sure, the day is full of other things and writing has to take a back seat. But taking a back seat isn't the same as falling off the tailgate.

Let's face it. People do the things they want to do, the things that give them pleasure and satisfaction. They put off the things they don't like to do, and they *make time* for the things they like to do.

Time is the stuff that nobody has enough of. Where does it all go? More to the point, how can you catch hold of some of it? Here's a little secret about time. Everybody's time is always filled. Nobody "has" time, at least not in the sense that people have money in the bank or food on the shelves. Time isn't something you save up and then use when something important comes along. Your time is always filled, always used. It's just a question of what you decide to use it for.

That point was brought home to me recently in an unusual manner. About four years ago, I decided to learn to play the banjo and began taking lessons from a teacher with unusual teaching skills. Now, a beginner at anything is in a very vulnerable state, but this teacher had me enjoying the banjo from the first lesson on. And do you know? Before I realized what was happening I was spending two to three hours a day practicing.

A year later a friend asked me how I found the time—and I had to give it a good think before I could answer. The truth was, I found the activity more satisfying than *other* activities. Since we always manage to find time for the things we like to do, I found the time for practicing the banjo. Twenty minutes here, half an hour there. Don't you do exactly the same thing when you're in the middle of an absorbing novel?

What's that you say? Why wasn't I writing instead of fooling around with a banjo? Gee, I didn't have the time.

The trick will be to make the act of writing satisfying in itself, regardless of the result or outcome of the writing.

Question. How can you make it more likely that you will make time for writing?

Answer. Fix it so that writing offers more satisfaction than other activities; fix it so that there are *immediate* (daily) successes, so that there is *joy* associated with the *act* of writing. Of *course* there will be carloads of kicks to be had when the writing is finished and appreciated by others. But that source of satisfaction is too far off in the future to help you now. What you need to do is to discover the joys, the rewards of *writing*, in addition to the joys of *having written*. You need to discover that there is satisfaction to be had from letting your fingers trickle over the keys without worrying about the melody. You need to discover what every musician knows: that the *playing* is at least as satisfying as the applause that comes from *having played*.

You need to discover the thrill of finally putting together a sentence that says it just the way you wanted to say it, and the absolute bang to be had from taking a bulky sentence and, by slashing a few words here and there, making the sentence sing. You need to be able to experience the rapture of being able to say what you have on your mind—without interruption from the yes-butters and without contradiction from the nit-pickers. (Ha! Did you notice that the line above has "yes-butters" in it? I just made that up. I just sat here letting the sentence flow and made that up. It isn't in my dictionary. I created it. It may not be much, and it may not survive the editor, but I *created* it to serve a purpose. Oh, joy!) [*What the heck. "Yes-butters" stays. Ed.*]

And the harder you find the writing, the more joy you will find in the immediate successes that come from turning a satisfying phrase, in simplifying a sentence, in saying your piece. The more determined you are to make those words come out, the more delight will flow over you when something clicks into place.

So it isn't only the "having written" that can trigger fulfillment and satisfaction; it is the very act of writing itself. Later on I'll show you some ploys and devices to help provide a full menu of daily rewards for your efforts.

As for time, you've got as much as everyone else. And if you could find only enough to write two pages a day, those would add up pretty fast. Two pages a day for a month is forty pages, and that doesn't even count weekends. Two or three months at that level of production and you'd have an entire first draft. At which point the hardest part is done.

I'm not creative

Let me tell you the secret of creativity. *Everyone* is creative. Some people are more creative than others, but everyone creates. Creating is the act of making something out of nothing. Wait, that didn't come out right. Let me try that again. Creating is bringing something into existence that wasn't there before. There, that's better. If you ever made a mud pie as a kid, you were creating. If you've ever written a letter, you've been a creative writer. If you've ever made a meal in a kitchen, you've been a creative artist.

Let's cut this word "creative" down to size. Maybe because deities are often referred to as "Creators," the word has come to have intimidating overtones. Maybe because artists are referred to as "creative," we have the notion that only a special few can create. Not so. It may be that only a special few can do it *well,* but that's true of almost everything. So what? When you turn your thoughts into a set of words that someone else can understand, you are creating. And when you shape those words into something that informs, or teaches, or delights someone else, you are a successful creator. Notice that to be successful at your creating you don't have to be among the top three creative geniuses in the world. There's plenty of room for us lesser lights, and we can be just as useful or important or helpful to others as the top talents.

But make no mistake about it. Everyone creates. More talented and skillful people may create better, but everyone creates.

But I don't know how

You don't say! Have you ever written any letters? *That's* writing. Have you ever written memos? *That's* writing. Ever written a report? Or a thesis? Or a note to the milkman? *That's* writing, too.

The fact is that you *do* know how to write. You may not know how to organize, or how to decide what to put in and what to leave out. But you have a fundamental writing skill to build on.

People say, "I don't know how to spell, and I never learned the rules of grammar," and then leap to the conclusion that they can't write a book or anything else. Balderdash! Let me tell you something. It is *humanitarian* not to know the rules of grammar! Holy smoke! If we all knew the rules of grammar we'd put thousands of editors out of work. [*Thanks for the plug. Ed.*] And if nobody wrote books, good, bad, or otherwise, all those critics would have to go out and look for honest work.

There's no denying that writing can be hard work. There's no denying that you may have to struggle for a long time to get that problem page to work right. You may even have to struggle, as I often do, to get a single sentence to come out right. But struggling with writing isn't the same as not being able to write at all.

Oh, yes. You already know how to write, just as you already know how to speak. You may not be a polished public speaker, but if you wanted to be one you certainly wouldn't be starting from square one.

So, you already *are* a writer—you just aren't yet a writer of books.

Who am I to write about this subject?

Good question. How dare you think that you know something that someone else would like to know? Where do you get off thinking that you have something to share that others might appreciate? Of course, if you are not a physicist, it probably would be presumptuous to write a physics text. If you are not a plumber it might be arrogant to write a book on plumbing.

Notice I said "might." How could you write a medical book if you aren't a doctor? Maybe you've had some unnerving experiences as a patient and want to share them with others. Maybe you were a patient, and, being an architect, you want to make recommendations for hospital design. Maybe you want to write a story with a medical setting. There are lots of possibilities.

Frankly, it never occurred to me to write *this* book. There are hundreds of books on how to write—and who am I to write about this subject?

But events conspired. Once, after giving a talk to a group of trainers, two or three people seemed fascinated with my comments about how I shape a manuscript. I couldn't imagine what was so interesting to them. Heck, I thought, doesn't *everyone* test a manuscript until it does what he or she wants it to do? Not two weeks later someone said I ought to write a book for people who want to write a book but who don't know how to make it work. Very flattering, I thought, but who am *I* to write such a book?

A month or two later I had a request from a trainer in a large corporation. "We'd like to record you describing your procedure for writing a book. We think our new writers will find it useful.

Besides, there are a lot of people who want to know some of the more personal things about writing." Personal things, I asked? "Yes. You know, some of the things that give you trouble, the stumbling blocks, and what you do about them." Gee, I thought, who am *I* to write about a thing like that? Besides, who would want to read it? And then I caught myself in mid-thought, having realized that I was running through all the negative thoughts that are *sure* to stop anyone from writing (or from doing almost anything else). I was astonished at having caught myself in a spiral of self-defeating thoughts, because I knew I had devised some *positive* ways to get the writing done when I needed to. There and then I decided to begin collecting my thoughts.

Having learned that the best memory is one that is written down, I started a folder labeled "The How-to-Write-a-Book Book," and began stuffing notes into it every now and again. At that point I still hadn't resolved to write a book, didn't have any idea what it might contain, and certainly didn't know if the folder label might turn out to be the title. But a few months later, a scientist contacted me. He worked at a local electronics company and thought he'd take a chance and call, even though we were strangers. What did he want? Well, he said hesitantly, he had published a number of papers in scientific journals and had written a number of monthly reports, and now he was thinking of writing a book. Could I give him some advice? *Me?* He wanted advice on writing from *me*? I, who had always thought of myself as a nonwriter? I was astonished. What could I tell him that he didn't already know?

Well, during that conversation I learned that there was quite a bit he didn't know. For example, when I asked him who the book was going to be *for*, he replied, "Gee, I never thought of that." And when I asked him what he thought he wanted the book to *do*, he said he hadn't thought about that, either. It was at that moment that a little seed of an idea grew in my consciousness. "Maybe I *am* somebody to presume to write such a thing. Maybe there *are* other people just like me. Maybe they want to write, or feel they ought to write, but something is holding them back. Maybe I'm not the only one who doesn't do things for the darnedest reasons. And if there *are* people like that, then maybe I am the person to take a whack at helping them out. Not with advice on style and structure, but on how to get it down and how to make it work."

So I tucked a few more notes into the folder—and put it away. But from then on, whenever I sat down at the typewriter I thought about the way I was feeling, about the problems I was facing, and about the solutions I was using. And I would add another note or two to the folder—and put it away again.

One by one the pages were slipped into the folder. First just a paragraph, and then an entire page. Before long there were twenty pages. Disconnected, but twenty pages! Why, that's a good start on a book. So I told myself a Positive Ploy: "You've already got twenty pages of a draft. You're already well along the way and only have a few more pages to go." That statement initiated the "Working on the Book" ritual. I prepared a three-ring binder, inserted dividers and a piece of cardboard for front and back (to make it look thicker), and was on my way. But more about those ploys later.

Then one day, while nearing the end of the first draft, there was a sudden twinge in my headbone. "Who are *you* to be writing about writing a book?" it said. Suddenly I had visions of English teachers and "real" writers laughing at my work and deriding my arrogance in thinking I could write about writing. Right there my fingers froze on the keyboard, and would you believe it? I quit! I gave up. I put it away—and didn't touch it again for two years. Finally I began working on it again, thanks to the urging of some good friends. But even after finishing the first draft, I fell into the same trap: I quit, and put it away again, for the same reason—for three more years.

The point is that you are not alone with your self-doubts about the value of what you have to say; you're only one among millions. Who am I to say whether I'm the one to write a book about writing a book? Nobody! It's for me to *write* it and for *you* and other readers to say whether I had any business writing it.

Who are *you* to say whether you are the one to write a book about that subject you've been thinking about? Nobody! It's for you to write it and for others to say whether they find it of value.

How can you keep from quitting before you start? First off, tell yourself that it's O.K. to have self-doubts. It's O.K. to be nervous about the value of your project. If famous actors can get stage-fright it's O.K. for you to get finger-fright.

Next, tell yourself that everybody has to start someplace. An anonymous writer once said, "The first page of *War and Peace* was once blank: Tolstoy filled it in." He didn't *have* to. He could have sat there wringing his hands and thinking thoughts like, "Gosh, who am *I* to write about war and peace? Maybe I'd better forget the whole thing." Tolstoy didn't know whether it was going to be a success *before he wrote it*. Nobody knows for sure. So what?

Then, tell yourself that you are writing only for yourself. Tell yourself that nobody is going to see what you are writing and that therefore you can write anything you please. In any *way* that you please. Sure, it's hard. If it weren't, a lot more people would be doing it. But it isn't impossible, it isn't against the law, it isn't fattening, and it isn't an activity reserved for a chosen few.

Finally, tell yourself that it doesn't matter much what you write down, as long as you write *something*, because you know the secret for making your writing do what you want it to do (which you will before you finish this book).

What would people say!

Oh, gosh yes! What *would* they say! What would your English teacher say? What would your old professor say? What would the critics say? (Grovel, grovel.)

You think you're alone in that thought? Not for a minute. A great deal of our behavior is controlled by thoughts of "What would they say?" I don't know why, but it is. People don't buy the suit or dress they really like because of what they think other people would say. They don't take up the hobby they're interested in because of what they think other people would say. Sometimes they don't even marry the person they love because of what they think other people would say. Whatever causes this attitude, there's a lot of it going around.

Of course the kindly thoughts and esteem of others are important to us. We want to look good in their eyes. But to live our lives on the basis of *guesses* about what people might say—about something we haven't even *done* yet—is, well, it's a form of slavery, that's what it is. And slavery is against the law!

There is a way out of this trap. First, tell yourself that others aren't ever going to *see* what you are writing, until you know for sure that it will interest them, and so what they might think about it *now* doesn't matter worth a darn. And that's the truth.

Next, tell yourself that nobody is going to *hear* about what you are writing until it is written down. If you spend time *telling* people about what you are writing, two or three things may happen. The first is that you will lay yourself open to hearing all the reasons it won't work, shouldn't be done, or shouldn't be done by you. There is no way that you will be able to explain what you are doing so that others will see it in their minds the way you see it in yours, so why ask for trouble? If people ask what you are writing about, do as I do: tell them you haven't figured it out yet.

Once you're well along in the project, it is appropriate to try out bits and pieces of your writing on one person or another, both as a means of helping to get it clarified and to break log jams. But that's very different from telling people about your project before you begin, or before you are far enough along to know that you will finish no matter what people say.

The second thing that can happen if you describe the details of your writing project to others is that your mind will finish with it. Psychologists talk about "closure," meaning that getting it off your chest gives your mind a chance to be done with it. And you don't want to be done with it until it is on paper. So tell people you are "writing something," but keep the details to yourself.

There's a third reason to keep it to yourself, and that's to keep it from being stolen. There are a lot of people who would be happy to steal your ideas, many of whom don't even think of it as stealing. If they think of it as a good idea their (pea) brain tells them either that *they* thought of it a long time ago, or that it is just common sense and therefore not your property. Don't take the risk. Just keep your mouth closed and your fingers moving.

Another ploy for beating the "What would they say!" trap is to write only for a loved one or a very trusted friend. Tell yourself that you are writing only for that person. Since you are writing for people you really trust, you don't have to worry about what they will say. They will be kind, they will be appreciative, and they will reward you with warm fuzzies just for going to the trouble of writing it, good or not.

Give yourself those messages and the "What will people say!" monster will shrink to a size you can boot across the room.

It would never be published

This is a real pretzel of an obstacle. You haven't even written it yet, don't know yet what it will contain or what it will look like, but already you know it won't be published. Such clairvoyance! Such predictive power! Such hogwash!

It could be true, though. It's quite possible nobody will want to publish it. But that isn't a good enough reason for quitting before you start. And if thoughts about the impossibility of getting your book published bother *you*, here's what to do about it.

First, tell yourself that you don't care whether it will be published or not. In fact, tell yourself that you won't even *think* about publishers while you are writing.

Second, tell yourself that if you like the finished product, it *will* be published, because *you* are going to publish it yourself. You can, you know. Tell yourself that since you are going to publish it yourself *you* will be the one who decides what it will contain and how it will look. If a publisher shows interest in it once the book is written, fine. But with or without a publisher clamoring for your book, it will be published by *someone*.

Third, remind yourself that there are several forms of "publishing." When I wrote that piece for the soldiers and ran it off on a mimeograph machine, that was a form of publishing. It wasn't printed by a real publisher, but it was printed (sort of), and it was distributed to those who needed it. When you write a Christmas letter and send it out, that's a form of publishing, too. To publish means to make it public, even though often the "public" that sees it is very limited.

Finally, tell yourself that by the time you have finished your book and gone through the steps I'll outline later, there is at least one publisher that *will* want to publish it.

With those ploys in mind the who-will-want-to-publish-it obstacle will simply lie down and die.

A little experiment

Before you move on to the next chapter, I'd like you to try a little experiment. Write down what you consider to be the one thing that most keeps you from starting your book. It might be one of the items I've just discussed, or it might be another. Write it down here.

____

____

Now imagine that a friend of yours came to you and said, "You know, I think I'd like to write a book, but I can't because

____,” and then fill in the blank with what you just wrote down. How would you reply to your friend? What would you say that would help him or her to get started? Go ahead, say it out loud.

Sounded pretty convincing, didn't it? So say the same thing to yourself. Say it every morning whether you are writing or not, and you will have at least one Positive Ploy working for you.

In sum

Yes, there are lots of excuses for not writing, and lots of reasons for quitting before you finish. But there are ways of stepping over these obstacles; some have been described in this chapter, and others will follow. You can use them to help build your resolve to get started, to strengthen your spirit for getting it down.

Everyone tilts at the windmills of self-doubt; some people win, some lose. Now that you know there are ploys and strategies for winning, it's time to get on with it. So let's get that book written.

Girding the Loins

Many forces push and pull at the writer, whether that writer is a novice or a pro: problems of the day, the things that need doing, the telephone, the kids, the thoughts about next month's vacation. All these and more try to steal the mind of the writer from the task at hand. The trick is to make as many of the forces as possible work *for* you rather than against you. The trick is to create a force-field that pushes you *toward* your writing rather than away from it. That is done by arranging the physical and the emotional writing environment, and by writing during the time that works for you.

In the preceding chapter, I tried to help you neutralize the negative forces caused by wrong ideas about writing. Now we will plot and scheme toward creating a writing world that will cheer you on, that will make you feel good when you write, and that will contain the minimum number of distractions. Since we need all the help we can get, we don't want to overlook a single possibility.

The writing place

If you find it difficult to write standing up, you'll have to find a place to sit down. No, that's not meant to be funny. I know managers who work at stand-up desks, and you may know some too. They say it keeps the blood flowing and the meetings short. So think about your best writing position and prepare accordingly.

You need a place where you can spread out some papers and not worry that they will be "neatened up" by a passing cleaning-mobile (i.e., someone suffering from tidymania). It needs to *look* like a writing place, and it needs to have all the things you will need for the task at hand. Such a place will help trigger writing thoughts, and it will help serve notice to others that you are not to be disturbed.

Some people think that a good writer can write anywhere and feel that fixing up a place is an unnecessary ritual. Maybe so. I'm sure there are writers who can write underwater. But I'm not one of them, and neither are a lot of other folks. I go to great lengths to make my writing place just right, and if you think it will help you to get at it, then you should too.

What if you spend a lot of time in hotel rooms, because you travel in your work? Certainly you have the *time* to write, even

A REAL writer smirks at his standup desk.

if you don't have your *place* to write. What to do? Handle it as a colleague of mine does: work on a topic rather than on the entire book. Rather than try to write the next few pages, expand a note, or flesh out an idea. Focus on a small piece rather than on the whole, and you should be able to make the time productive even though the place isn't ideal. This tactic won't get the entire book written, of course, but it can get you so tantalizingly close that the quality of your writing space will take a back seat as an obstacle to writing.

Just because you don't have a super place to write is no excuse *not* to write, though. A proper place will help you along, but if you tell yourself that you're not writing because you don't have an ideal place for it, you're just goofing off.

Once you begin to write you, too, will become an expert on how to avoid it. You will sharpen pencils, get up for a cup of coffee, stare at the clouds, and probably do some things the rest of us haven't even thought of. That's O.K. It's warmup. Runners spend time warming up, as do most other people in the worlds

of sports, theatre, and music. They don't think of that as procrastinating; they think of it as necessary to getting in the mood, to loosening up.

But there's a limit to warming up. If you spend all day warming up, you'll have nothing to show but a bunch of pencils sharpened down to the nub. So organize your space to include the minimum number of things that you personally find distracting. Fix it so that it *looks* like a writing place, and so that just about everything you see when sitting there has something to do with your writing project—and nothing else.

Several years after I began writing, I finally constructed an L-shaped writing table for myself that has everything I need. It has space for notes, folders for obsolete draft pages, and all of the necessary utensils, such as pencils, paper, scissors, stapler, and glue. I don't have to get up out of my chair for *anything* I might need while writing, except coffee. Since I spend a lot of time gazing at the typewriter, I bought myself a comfortable executive office chair that swivels and that pushes me back toward the typewriter when I try to lean too far back in it. (Can you believe it? A pushy chair!) The desk faces a wall that is blank except for my progress chart (more on that later) and a small card headed, "Sayings for a Lonely Writer." Because I found myself wasting a lot of time hunting for a pencil that was always hiding under one unruly paper pile or another, I built a pencil holder and mounted it on the wall within easy reach. It holds four pencils rather than one, which eliminates *that* distraction.

My writing place is about as ideal as I can make it; I need all the help I can get.

It wasn't always thus. When I first started to write the kids were small and noisy and had no respect for Father the Writer. (Now they are grown and civilized, and very helpful.) I set up a writing place in one corner of a bedroom that was also being used as an office, and put the table under the window so I'd have a lot of light.

MY NEW BOOK: "HOW TO MAKE DECISIONS AND STICK BY THEM."
WHATTA YOU MEAN NEW? YOU WROTE THAT BOOK OVER A YEAR AGO.
– THE REVISED EDITION?

What a mistake *that* was. I had a lot of light, all right, but I also had a lot of distractions. There was a tree outside the window, and it became my duty to check the leaves each time I sat down to make sure they were all facing in the proper direction. After checking on the birds who plied their tree-squatting trade in this tree, I felt it necessary to count the droppings on the various branches, just to see if there was a trend, you see. Occasionally a piece of bark would fall off the trunk, at which time it became imperative to consider the inner workings of trunks. Since I had, and have, no intention of writing about trees, the window and the tree served only to interfere with the business at hand.

A writing place in your office is a special problem, because of the number and nature of the distractions. Phone calls, drop-in visitors, and administrivia are harder to control in the office than at home. For example, although it isn't a nice thing to do, at home you can get away with ranting and bellowing at those who encroach on your turf during writing time. You're not nearly so likely to get away with that at the office. Superiors won't stand for it, and subordinates will find ways to get even.

The key trick to making an office environment work as a writing place is to separate the office and the writing as completely as you can. Don't try to write at your main desk. Get another desk, or a table, and write where you can't see the work piled on your regular work desk. If you have a secretary, instruct that calls be held and visitors derailed during your writing time. If you don't have that luxury, unplug the telephone and close

B.C.

your door. If you can't turn off the phone, you can take a message and return the call later. If you don't have an office door, you can wear ear plugs and hang a sign on your back that says, "Do Not Disturb," or "Measles."

Another way to make an office writing space work is to write there when no one else is around. If the phone rings, you can ignore it. After all, you shouldn't answer a phone just because it rings. You should answer it only when it rings *and* you are ready to receive calls.

Think about what distracts *you* and then organize your space to minimize those distractions.

Things

Distractions are only one element of the writing environment; the feel of the "things" in that environment is another. Why use one color of paper if another one makes you feel good? Why use one type of paper if the feel of another type is pleasurable to the fingers? Why indeed? Since I spend a great deal of time staring at a typewriter, I decided to make it something pleasurable to stare at. I bought a new machine and had it painted a pleasant lemon color. Not everybody likes it, but then I don't care what *everybody* likes. What matters is arranging the writing environment to be as pleasing to *me* as possible. When I enter my office, the first thing I see is my bright lemon-colored typewriter beckoning me to come feel it (since the paint-job was done over the original paint, the finish is slightly wrinkled, and it feels good). You think that's kinky? I don't care. It helps me to get on with the act of writing.

Time

When is the best time to write? Morning? Afternoon? In the quiet of the evening? There isn't a single answer. The easy thing to say is that you should write during the time of day that is best for you. If you are a morning person, you should write during the morning and save the other activities for the remainder of the day. And so on.

But it isn't that easy, is it? You have to work for a living, there are social obligations, and there are chores to do. Then what? Then you think about your day and find a couple of hours that you can set aside for writing. *First* you find the time, and *then* you get yourself in shape for it. Suppose you think you can spend between 8–10 P.M. for writing, even though you'd rather write in the morning. You've had dinner, you've spent time with the family, and you've read the evening paper. But you're bushed. You've had a hard day, and you don't *feel* like writing. Right. Welcome to the club.

What to do? Two things. Get your body and your mind in shape. Spend ten minutes before dinner exercising. Run with the kids, play a little ball, or just leap around. That will loosen you up from the tensions of the day. After dinner, take a little nap if you feel like one. That will refresh your mind, and you'll be in better shape to write.

Then, at 8 P.M. sit down at your writing place and *don't get up* until 10. Even if you don't write a word. But you *will* write. Especially if you have "idea" notes. The first few minutes or even the first hour may seem wasted because "nothing comes," but that's just warmup time. Try not to worry about it. The main thing is to make yourself fit and to set up a schedule that you keep. In the next chapter, I'll show you how to get started, how to make the muse strike.

Writing time, however, is not the same as idea time. Though you may spend two hours each day writing, you may spend considerably more time in thinking about what to write. *Any time* is *idea* time, and since ideas may pop into your head at the oddest moments, it pays to carry a small notebook or some three-by-five-inch cards. Those ideas and notes will help you get started in whatever space you have to work in.

How long should you write at a sitting? Set a reasonable amount of time that you can realistically expect to have, and then write *at least* until that minimum time is up. If you're hot, keep going until you run out of steam. But don't quit until that minimum time is up. If you *know* that nothing will prevent you from spending that time sitting there for your allotted time, whether you are productive or not, you might as well become productive. Knowing that you will sit for a minimum time will help get you into the habit of turning off the world and turning on your project. That isn't always easy, but the rule of "minimum writing time" helps.

When I am writing something, I write from 8:30 A.M. until noon, rain or shine. I don't answer the phone, I don't interrupt myself to take care of a chore or two, and I don't talk to family. I put a hostile sign on the door and then close it. I write in the mornings now because I can afford to buy that time for myself. When I first started to write I couldn't do that because I was working for someone else. I had to write during evenings and weekends. But I did the same thing: set up a time, sat down, and didn't get up until the minimum time had passed—or until I had written my quota of pages. (More on that later.)

Find your time and then stick to it. If the amount of writing you do for the first day or week doesn't thrill you, *be thrilled about the fact that you are sticking with it.* Rejoice at your perseverance.

Cooperation

Now then, it is one thing to resolve to make time to write; it may be quite another to arrange for "time out" from the world. It is one thing to arrange to spend two hours each day trying to write; it is something else to get *other* people to allow you to spend two hours trying to write.

How can you cause the world to stop beating a path to your head? I have a number of suggestions, the main one being to set up a "writing place" and to broadcast the rule that nobody is to disturb you while you are sitting there. Put a sign on the back of your chair saying "Writer at Work," or "Do Not Disturb," or something even nastier if needed. Wear a special hat that says you are in the writing mode. Wear a brightly-colored scarf; put up a flag. Do whatever you can think of to make it clearly visible to all concerned that you are writing. Close the door. Lock it.

Then, if people *do* have the nerve or the insensitivity to disturb you, ignore them. Pretend they are not even there. Maybe they will go away. If they don't, react. Not politely. Irrationally. Growl, grimace, and grunt. Holler that you were interrupted just at your most creative moment. Throw a tantrum. After all, creative people are *supposed* to be temperamental; use that myth to your advantage. Threaten family members that if they keep butting in, you may have to let them go.

If you *do* have to interrupt yourself with some pressing chore—say, taking out the garbage—do it clumsily. Drop it on the floor.

But let people know that they cannot interrupt you with immunity, without risk. Let them know that if they interrupt you, they bloody well better be ready to suffer the consequences. Then, if interrupted, lay on the consequences!

Though it may be fun to rant and rave and throw an occasional tantrum, these actions are not winners of friends. They may help keep the world at bay, but you don't want to run the risk that it will stay at bay permanently. So always use the positive approach whenever you can. You can do that by making your writing a family project. Get everyone in on the act. Make a deal with them to the effect that if they will help you create the proper environment, you will do something in return. Do what? I dunno. What would they like? A day in the country? A day in the city? A mention in the book? A night on the town? A chocolate sundae? Ask *them*. Then set up a way to make their progress toward that goal *visible*. Put a chart on the wall that shows the number of hours of time and quiet they have contributed. Put a red line at the point you intend to offer something in return.

Draw a new point on the chart every day. And then when the curve reaches the red line, pay off! Rejoice. Tell them how much help they are and how much they are contributing to the project. Tell them how much you appreciate their assistance. Distribute some hugs and kisses. Then draw another payoff line on the chart and start all over again—until you can wave at them the pages you have created with *their* help and forbearance.

Now that you've gathered the forces and started them working for you, it's time to start writing.

Peanuts / *Charles Schulz*

Striking the Muse

Having firmed the resolve, prepared a place, and instructed the family, it is time to begin. But where? There is that blank piece of paper, beckoning. What should you write first? How do you start?

"Start with an outline," they used to say—over and over again.

"After I've approved your outline you may begin writing your theme."

"Begin with a topic sentence, and then complete the paragraph. Write a topic sentence for the next paragraph, and so on."

"Never write a paragraph that has only one sentence in it."

"And never start a sentence with *and*."

Bullbleep!

Whatever writing is, it certainly isn't something that has to start with an outline—*or* a topic sentence. It *might* start there, if that's what you feel like doing. But it doesn't *have* to start there. It will be organized before it is finished, but it doesn't have to be organized when you begin. As a matter of fact, many writers use the act of writing as the main way to think through what it is they want to say. Though they may be clear on the topic, they may not be clear on the scope of the book, or on the main emphasis, or even on what will go where. So they put some words on paper and push them around, much as one might push furniture around a room to see where it fits best.

So the secret to getting started is to ignore the rules! Write the first thing that comes to your hand. Never mind about outlines, or sense, or tense, or topic sentences. Just get some words down on that paper. You can never fix what isn't there, so the first step is to pour the spaghetti of the mind onto that piece of paper.

First you get it down, and then you get it good

If you have already outlined what you want to say, go ahead and start at the beginning. But remind yourself that there is no reason to start at the beginning other than that is where you happen to feel like writing at the moment. I have a collection of writers' sayings on the wall in front of me. One says, "The last thing we decide in writing a book is what to put first."

It's true. If the body of the book isn't crystal clear in your mind when you sit down to write the introduction (and there is no reason why it should be), that introduction will be very difficult to write. So why sit there stewing over an introduction for a book that hasn't been written yet? No reason at all.

If you don't have to start at the beginning, where *do* you begin? Anywhere your head happens to be. First you get it down, and then you get it good. The object is to write. Having written, it is then possible to shape it into the book you want it to be. Just as you can't sculpt a beautiful marble figure until you have the marble, you can't polish writing that isn't written. So the first goal is writing. Not clear writing, or amusing writing, or articulate writing, but writing.

The musemyth

Have you ever heard someone say, "I can write only when the muse strikes," or "I could produce more if the muse would strike more often"? These people either believe that writing is done only when some mystical door to the "creative self" is opened, or they are using it as an excuse to goof off. They also seem to believe that there is nothing they can do to open that door. They're wrong.

There are any number of ploys that can be used to make the muse strike. The trick is to understand clearly what you are shooting for. Sometimes, when people say, "The muse didn't strike," they mean they couldn't get started producing. Other times they mean they didn't have an idea to write about. You must keep in mind that production is the goal. If you can find ways to make yourself write that daily quota of pages, the ideas will come. Get the fingers started and the mind will follow.

Sure, we all have bad days. But that doesn't alter the fact that you can make yourself get going. Muse, my foot. The muse strikes those who strike the muse.

Have you ever heard stories about great problems solved by great inventors? They tell us that they solve problems by gathering all the information they can, and then mull it, massage it, worry it, fondle it, and forget it. The brain is like many other organs that continue to work even when we don't pay attention to it. And sometimes when we least expect it, the solution appears. It doesn't appear because we were standing at a bus stop waiting for solutions, or because we stared off into space. It appears because we thought about it, noodled about it, made notes about it, and wrote about it.

And that's how you strike the muse. You fix up your place, set your schedule, and begin by attaching the seat of your pants to the seat of the chair. Then write something. Anything. Here are some ploys to show you how to get yourself started.

Stream of consciousness

Having trouble getting started? Try this. Type (or write) what is going on in your head.

"What in the world am I doing here killing myself over a few thousand lousy words. If I had any sense I'd be out playing. As it is, here I am trying to write about ______________________."

"That was a late night and I'm finding it hard to concentrate. How in the world can anyone expect me to be able write about ______________________?"

Drivel? Sure, but it gets you started. Keep the words coming and the mind will follow along. If you feel like it, be more hostile. Don't forget: *nobody* is going to see this first draft. Absolutely no one.

"All right, you worthless bums, here is what I'm trying to tell you about. If you had any sense you would realize that this is important stuff. What is? Well, I'm trying to tell you about ______________________."

Silly? Maybe the *words* are silly. But they are as good as gold if they help to get you started.

Write a letter

Here is a ploy to get you around the "What will people say" bogeyman and get your fingers started at the same time. Write a letter to a kindly, trusted friend about what you are trying to write about, or about what you are stuck on (the problem you haven't been able to solve). If you don't have such a friend, make one up. You don't have to mail the letter—just write it.

When I first started writing, I had a terrible time getting started. I had no idea how one went about writing a book, and I had trouble almost every day in getting the fingers moving. Worse, I thought that as soon as "real writers" sat down, the sparks flew and they wrote up a storm.

Real Writers have since told me that I have a crazy sense of reality (few people realize just how hard the pros work to get where they are), but that crazy image made it even harder to get started. Eventually I set up the daily page quota and vowed not to get out of my chair until it was met.

Great! I had a quota, but I still had the problem of getting started each day to fill it. Once I realized that what you write first isn't the same as what you write last, and that nobody has to see what you write first, things improved. I told myself that I would fill my quota with writing even if I had to write letters. And in the beginning I *did* have to write letters once in a while to get started. I would start a letter like this:

> *Dear Dave:*
>
> *Look, dammit! This isn't going the way I wanted it to. I'm not sure which section should be in the middle and which at the end. Let me tell you what the sections contain.*

Or

> *Dear Dave:*
>
> *Yesterday I typed myself into a box. It started out all right, but then I got strangled by details. Let me tell you what I'm trying to say. It's this.*

And it worked. In the early days I actually mailed a couple of these letters, and the replies (always gentle) would help even more.

But be careful. Go ahead and write a letter, but don't mail it unless you have a guaranteed, sure-fire friend who can be counted on for moral support rather than criticism. After all, you aren't writing these letters for constructive criticism; you are writing them as a means of getting yourself started. Period. So be absolutely certain you mail such letters only to someone you can trust with your inner soul. Anyone else will slow you down or totally destroy your will to continue.

Instead of mailing those letters, put them into a folder. Who knows? Maybe you will ultimately do a book of letters.

Expand your notes

By the time you sit down to write your book, you have probably built a folder of notes. If your folder looks like mine it will have in it an assortment of envelopes, napkins, and paper place mats, all of which have on them a scribbled note or two. In addition, you may have a paragraph, or even a page, that you were motivated to write while you were thinking about doing the book. Furthermore, you are likely to have reference materials, examples, clippings, or cartoons that seem pertinent to the project.

This is great stuff to help you get started. Take one of the notes and expand it. Write it out in its entirety. Describe the essence of the note. Never mind if it is out of sequence, that it isn't related to the part of the book you are working on. Embellish the note and you will have gotten yourself started. In fact, writing the entire book can be a matter of expanding your notes until they are all strung together in a coherent manner.

"I'm writing a story, but I can't think of what to put after 'Once Upon A Time.' "

Quote a quote

One way to get started is to let someone else do it for you. Having trouble with that blank piece of paper? Paste a quotation on it and it won't be blank anymore. And while you're cutting and pasting, your mind will start turning to the project at hand.

I used this ploy in earlier days. I had kept a collection of friends' utterances that tickled me. (For example, "I'm getting sick and tired of being sick and tired.") One day I had a great idea! I would start each chapter with one of these witty sayings. It was great fun poring through the folder for just the right one, and then typing it at the head of the chapter. It didn't have anything to do with anything, and I later took them out for that reason. But they were very useful—they got me started.

Clip a cartoon

Most of my books have at least one Snoopy cartoon in them. With permission, of course. Cartoons are sometimes a good way to emphasize a point, break up the page and make it more interesting, or to lighten up the tone.

Of course, you can't slip a cartoon into your manuscript just because it strikes you as funny. It needs to be there to make a point, to poke fun at a point, or to underline a point. There needs to be some text to insert the cartoon into.

And there is another ploy to get you started. Write the text that the cartoon relates to. Think about what you would have to write to make that cartoon just right, and then write that part of the book. Maybe only a page—but who cares? It gets you started.

State your purpose

When you have trouble, try stating your purpose. Or restating it if you have done it before. Write down what the book is about and what you want it to accomplish, and it will get you off dead center. You will have to do it before you are too far into the project, anyhow, so use it as a ploy to get you started when you are stuck.

It isn't good enough merely to say, "This is a book about ____________________." You already know that. What you may not have clearly in mind is the effect you want to have on your readers. Do you want them to learn something? If so, say what you want them to be able to do when they finish the book. Say it in as much detail as you can muster. Do you want to inform? What information do you want to include? How about a few examples of things that definitely should be left out?

Your purpose may change as you write, and that is another good reason to restate it once in a while. By the time I finish a book, I may have a dozen pages or more on which I summarized the purpose, the scope, the content, the sequence, or any other aspect I felt would help clarify the big picture.

You may be asking, "If it's so important to state a purpose, shouldn't you *begin* by doing that? Good question. You will have to know your purpose before you shape the *final* version of the book, of course, but you can do a lot of writing without having that purpose honed to precision, and you may need to do a lot of writing as the means of finding out just exactly what purpose makes sense. It's more important to *begin*, though, than to begin at the beginning. If you can clarify the purpose right off, fine. But don't feel compelled to begin there. Write a summary of your purpose when you are stuck. Do it every time you are stuck.

Write a review

Here is a dandy way to get yourself started: write a review of the book you are going to write. Sound odd? Try it once and see if it doesn't get you off dead center. It doesn't matter that the review may not be literate, accurate, or even grammatical. It doesn't even matter if you use glowing superlatives you would never use in ordinary conversation. Just go ahead and review this fantastic new book. Say what is good about it and why people would want to read it. Go into as much detail as you want, and don't worry about whether the review is properly organized. Just let it out.

> You wouldn't believe how clearly this book explains the subject of ________________. Why, it is astounding! Fantabulous! It begins with ________________________, and then talks about ______________________________. After that, etc.

Write a review and you may discover that you have written a nice statement of purpose. At the very least, you got started. At most, you may have some great paragraphs to include in your letter to a publisher about why the book should be published.

Describe your audience

Having trouble getting started today? Can't think of where or how to begin? O.K. Take a little time out and write something about the audience you are writing for. Don't say your audience is "everybody." That's unrealistic. Also impossible. You sat down there because you wanted to write about something. Fine. Who is to reap the benefit of your writing? Managers? Teachers? Parents? Computer hobbyists? Poetry fanciers? Who are they and what are they like?

Write everything you know about them. Write down their age range, their occupation(s), and what you know about the sort of hobbies they may pursue. Say what you know about their attitudes, their biases, their education. If you find you don't know anything about your audience, or even who that audience is, you will have discovered one of the reasons you are having difficulty getting started.

I'm sure you will agree that you would have a lot less trouble writing a letter to a good friend than one that began, "Dear Public." You might not have much to say in a personal letter, but you would know what content would be appropriate and you would know how to go about saying it. It's infinitely harder to write to strangers. That's one reason it is harder to write business letters to "Dear Sir" than personal letters to "Dear Sue."

Somewhere along the line (the sooner the better) you are going to have to think deeply about your audience. The first time you have trouble getting started may be a good time to start on the written description of those you are trying to influence or inform.

This matter of the target audience is so important that it warrants a few more words. Your audience will have, or should have, an influence on how you write. It will have an influence on the language you use, on the examples you include, on the length of your sentences, and on their formality or informality. It's like tailoring a suit: you can build a suit to fit a lot better if you know the size and shape of the suitee. And you can get into trouble if you don't take the time to determine the nature of your audience.

For example, if you have ever read a computer manual that seemed to be written more for the expert programmer than for the user, you understand the importance of knowing, and writing for, your intended audience.

If you can't write at least a page or two about your intended audience, you will need to take time out to find out about them. How? Find some of them. Chat with them. The more you know about them the better you will be able to shape your project to accomplish its purpose.

Start a piece of paper headed "Audience" or "Reader" and keep it handy. Add to it whenever you think of something else you know about them. It will help the fingers to move.

Dangle a sentence

Ever get a letter that started in the middle of a sentence? My friends sometimes do, from me.

Dear Dave:
, which explains why I was thinking of you this morning.

So it's eccentric. I don't care. Why do it? Because sometimes I will think up a good phrase, or the last part of a sentence, before I think of the first part. And since I don't want to lose it before it gets away, I get it down.

Maybe the practice is a slopover from the getting-started ploy of ending the writing day in the middle of a sentence. If you dangle a sentence, you can easily get yourself started the next day by completing the sentence. If you can't keep yourself from finishing the sentence, by all means finish it. And then write something, such as, "Tomorrow the next section (or paragraph) will ______________________________," and let it dangle. The next day you begin by finishing the sentence.

Summing up

You can begin anywhere; there is no law that says you have to begin at the beginning or that the finished writing has to look like the first writing.

Anything that you can do to get yourself started is fair game; there is no law that says you are "bad" if you deliberately engage in windup activities, in false starts, or in self-congratulation for imagined success.

Good writing follows poor writing; first you get it down and then you get it good. You can't improve what isn't there. So get it down.

Staying With It

A few years ago, as part of a learning experiment, I set out to teach myself to ride the unicycle. Every afternoon after work I would try valiantly to mount my wheel, and then would run (or crawl) to the typewriter to make notes on daily progress. But for weeks and weeks there just wasn't any progress to report. It was disheartening, and several times I almost gave up.

When I finally learned to ride the darned thing about two months later, I reviewed my notes and made an astonishing discovery. I was reporting progress all along, but didn't know it! Thinking that progress could be measured only in terms of the *length of the ride*, I had kept reporting "no progress." But I had also made note of the number and location of the daily bruises, and on the methods I had tried for mounting the thing (it's something like trying to mount a greased balloon).

Though for a long time the length of the daily ride was zero inches, I could have reported progress all along if I had only known what to look for. When I moved from the rope in the garage to the backyard, that was progress. When today's bruises were fewer than yesterday's, that was progress. When the bruises began moving from the ankle toward the crotch, that was progress. When the unicycle flew shorter and shorter distances away after a fall, that was progress, too. And when I finally started riding, I could have put a protractor under my armpit to measure the angle of dangle, because the more skilled I became the less I needed my arms as balancing poles.

The point of this story is that as long as I defined progress *only* in terms of the length of the ride, that is, in terms of the "finished product," I could tell myself that I was making progress only *after* I had learned to ride. Until then I had to tell myself I was a total failure. That can be demoralizing, and it can lead to quitting.

Writing isn't much different from riding a unicycle. Though the ultimate success appears when the writing is finished, there is a lot of time and effort in between: time to become demoralized, time to have second thoughts, and time to quit. But there are also a lot of indicators of progress that can be used to spur you on, to fan your enthusiasm, and to use as reasons for rejoicing. When you are staring at your first—or hundredth—blank page, the finished product can seem farther away than a Martian mermaid. But if you know how to recognize the components of progress, you won't have to wait until the book is done to feel good about it—you can provide yourself with daily rewards.

The trick is to measure your progress from *yesterday*, rather than to measure the distance yet to travel. If you look only at how much is left to do, you may overwhelm yourself before you get too far off the starting block. But if you can focus on what you've done since yesterday, you will be able to sustain yourself. Just as a building is constructed one brick at a time, a book is constructed one page at a time. Think about the bricks you've put in place since yesterday, and the task will seem far more manageable than thinking about the bricks yet to be laid.

Here are some ways to do it.

Make a chart

Make a chart to record the number of pages you write each day. Show total number of pages along the vertical line and days along the horizontal line. Then draw a line that represents the number of pages that you intend to write each day—your self-imposed quota. I've always used four pages per day as my quota. When I exceed it I rejoice; when I don't, I still tell myself that I've done a good day's work and that I'm right on schedule. Don't give yourself a higher quota than you can fill. If you can easily write ten pages a day, set your quota at eight. If you find two pages a burden, set it at one. If you find it easier to set your expectations in terms of points to be made, arguments or examples to describe, do so. But set a quota, and then sit there until that quota is met. One way or another.

Put the chart on the wall in front of you, and then when you get up from each day's writing session, put a dot on the chart to show your progress for the day. Do it with a flourish, and tell yourself you are a good person because you have made progress since yesterday and therefore have moved closer to the finished book.

Be sure to count *all* the pages you drafted, not just the good ones. You're not conducting a scientific experiment that requires

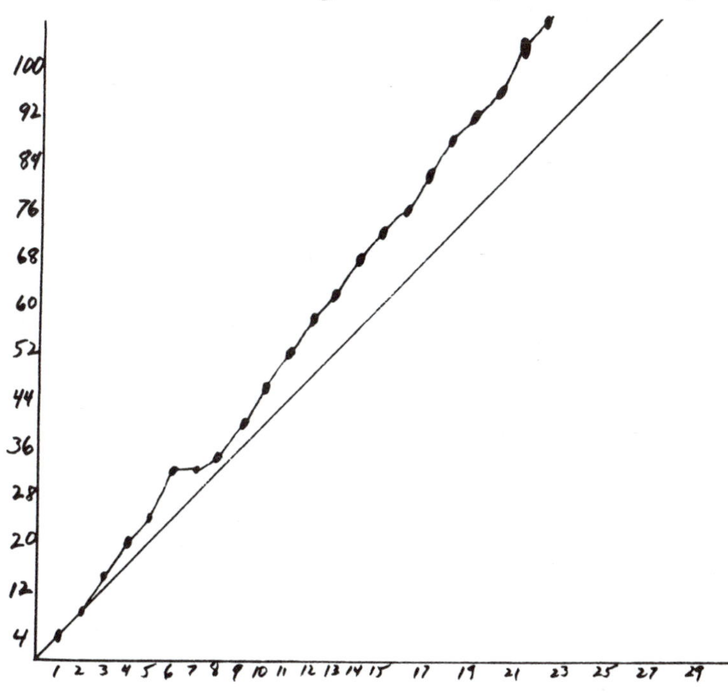

Use a progress chart as a way to reward yourself immediately after producing your daily quota of draft pages (it feels so goooood to make the little dot).

precise accuracy in the counting; you're trying to make yourself feel good enough about what you did today so that you will want to do it again tomorrow.

Fatten a folder

One of the most depressing things that can happen to those who find writing difficult is to throw a page into the wastebasket. Arrrrgh! It's like tearing off an arm and throwing it away. It's like casting off an old friend. And it feels like backward progress, since there is one page *less* than there was before. Oh, anguish! Oh, forlornity!

Fortunately, there is a solution. Don't throw anything away! You can use those obsolete pages as a terrific indicator of progress. Don't throw them away; put them into a folder. Label it "Obsolete pages" or "Pages nobody had enough sense to appreciate" or "Folder." It doesn't matter. Just save the pages and watch that folder grow. Put every obsolete scrap into it—pages that have been rewritten, old notes no longer needed. Tell yourself that one day you may use some of those pages in another manuscript. Tell yourself anything, but save them and you will reap two powerful advantages. First, you will no longer have to experience the anguish of throwing your own creations into the wastebasket. Second, you will use the fatness of the folder as an indicator of progress. The fatter it gets the closer you are to the end of the road.

This is an especially useful ploy because very often your manuscript will have fewer pages as you improve it. Your fattening folder of obsolete pages will counter the effect of the leaner manuscript. Folder fatness is an indicator of progress.

Make a book

It's a long way from the first blank page to the finished book, and anything you can do to make the distance seem shorter is worth doing. So start right out to make a book. Get a three-ring binder. There. You already have something that *looks* like a book. Now put two cardboard sheets in it, one in front, and one in back (to keep the pages from crinkling, you understand). Now add some tab pages to separate the chapters, and look at that! It's taking on the appearance of a book and it doesn't even have any pages in it yet! So what? If it makes you feel like staying with it, fine.

Now take some of your notes and slip them between the tabs about where you think those notes will be used as you write. You may want to add a page or two of notes here and there describing ideas you have, drawings you think you may want, or some of the paragraphs and pages you wrote while thinking about doing the book. Fiddle with it. Put a label or two on the tabs. They don't have to be chapter titles—maybe just a word to remind you of what that part will be about so you can find it more easily. Maybe just a number.

It won't be long before you have something that looks and feels like a book. All you have to do now is to rewrite some pages and expand some notes, right? We both know it isn't as simple as that. But so what? The object isn't to remind ourselves that writing is hard work. The object is to remind ourselves that writing is *possible*, and that you are making progress, by arranging things to make it look less formidable. So make it look like a book, and then take it one bite at a time.

Bulk it up

Here's a sneaky ploy to help you see some progress. Use fat paper. Don't use flimsy stuff; it takes too many pages to make a pile. Use heavier paper and you will be able to see the growth faster.

Here's another ploy. Use wide margins when you write. That puts less on a page and you will need more pages, and that will help the book to look fatter. If you need a justification (excuse) for wide margins, tell yourself that you should leave lots of room for editing and for notes. (That's true, by the way.) And be sure to double space; triple space if you have it. After all, you are trying to make it appear as though you have come a long way and only have a short way to go. If you can do that, you will be more likely to keep going.

This isn't just idle chatter. Psychologists refer to this phenomenon as the "end spurt." What it means is simply that we are more persistent near the end of a project than we are in the middle of it. Ever notice that the nearer you are to the end of a good book the less likely you are to put it down? That's end spurt. Ever notice that when you are almost done building those shelves you are more likely to stay with it, even though it's late at night? That's end spurt.

So bulk it up to make it look as though you're almost done.

Trigger a treat

You've decided on a writing schedule, on the time of day you will write, and on the amount of time you will devote to the daily session. Now you need to devise ways to make that resolve *pay off.* Not some time in the future when the book is finished. Now! You need to arrange to pay yourself for progress, using as currency any type of event or item that will make your world a little brighter.

Make an agreement with yourself promising that you will ______________________________ as soon as you have drafted ______ pages. This is technically known as contingency management; first you do *this*, and then you can have (or do) *that*. First you write a few pages, and then you will reward yourself by ______________________________. It doesn't have to be a large reward, but it needs to be something that *you* enjoy, and it needs to happen as soon as you have produced the agreed-upon number of pages.

What kinds of rewards? Whatever makes you feel good and/or whatever makes you feel good about yourself. First you write a page, and *then* you listen to a few minutes of music, enjoy a few pages from a book of cartoons, hug your spouse. Not before. Not during. *After.* If you are a chocolate-freak, you might consider making a glob or two contingent upon completing your daily ration of pages. Or make a telephone call to someone who understands what you are doing and report your daily progress. "Hey, I did my two pages today." Or three. Or whatever number you settle on.

Make good things happen as soon as you have drafted your daily quota, and the writing itself will begin to be more enjoyable. The laws of behavior tell us that if you pair two events closely in time, the first event (or act, or behavior) will begin to take on the reward value of the second. For example, if you like reading more than you like algebra, if you set up a rule that says, "First I'll do two algebra problems and *then* I'll read a few pages," the act of solving algebra problems will eventually become more pleasurable (move somewhat higher on the like-dislike scale). This arrangement can be made to work so well that eventually the act of solving algebra problems can be used as a reward for some other less-liked activity.

So be sure to make a list of the things you like to do and then do one of them after you have written your pages for the day. I seem to be hooked on eating (I do it every day), and so one of my ploys is to say "*First* I type my pages, and *then* I am entitled to lunch." More technically that works out to this: First I do the lower probability (less-liked) activity, and then I reward myself with some higher probability (better-liked) activity.

When I first started writing, I found even that arrangement too difficult. To say, "First you write your quota, and then you do something pleasurable" was like saying, "First you spend a lifetime being good, and then you'll go to heaven." The reward was too remote in time, and the amount of work required to get it was too much. What I needed, I decided, was to make myself feel good about any approximation toward writing. What I needed to do was to make myself feel good about sitting down to write, and then when I got myself into the habit of regularly sitting down to write, I could begin to reward myself for producing pages.

What I did was to make sure my writing place was the most comfortable place in the room. As I reported earlier, I built a typing table that is perfect for my needs, found that comfortable chair that tilts and swivels, and built a light fixture to hang over the typewriter. I made the pencil holder from some old brass cartridge cases. In other words, I built a place that I enjoyed being in, regardless of what I was doing there. And it worked, too. Since it felt good just to sit there, I sat there. The longer I sat, the more likely it was that the fingers would begin to move. And when they had moved long enough, they triggered a treat.

Lest the point be missed, let me lunge at it another way. The object is to find reasons to experience joy over the *act* of writing. And that means you can trigger a treat for sitting down, for just being persistent enough to stay your allotted time, for writing your daily quota, for turning a neat phrase or sentence that pleases you, for explaining a certain number of key points, for filling in a piece of the plot, or for finishing the first draft of a chapter. If you reward yourself for some of the hard work of writing, you will begin to make the *act* of writing as pleasurable as the *results* of that writing.

Leaping Obstacles

Keeping going involves more than just rewarding yourself for successive approximations (progress) toward the completed work. It involves being able to deal with a variety of obstacles along the way.

The Box

If you are new to writing, you will become well-acquainted with the Box. This is the thing you write yourself into when you begin a sentence and can't find a way out of. It is the state of temporary paralysis you find yourself in when there is no end to attach to the beginning. I know. I'm an expert. I've often started sentences only to get all tangled up, and then sat staring at the page trying to think of a way out.

There are solutions. Whenever you have trouble writing your way to the end of a sentence, there are three ploys to select from. One is simply to cross it out and start over. After all, there is nothing sacred about the sentence you started. Think of it as a false start. Better yet, tell yourself that it was a useful warmup (like jogging on the sidelines for a short time before starting a race), and *then* cross it out and start again.

The second ploy is the period. Very useful item, the period. When you are all tangled up in a sentence, use a period and make two sentences out of it. The sentence was probably too complicated, anyway.

The third solution is to let it dangle and move on to the next one. Make a pencil mark in the margin to remind yourself to come back to it later, leave some space, and then just let it sit there stewing in its own juice.

You can spend a great deal of time staring at tangled sentences. You can also beat this obstacle into a pulp by taking firm action against it. Junk it and start over, skewer it with a period, or leave it there and move on.

Short paper

If you already know exactly what you want to write about and how it will be organized—that is, if you don't have difficulty marshalling your thoughts—please skip over this section, because you'll never understand how short paper can be an obstacle to writing.

The usual piece of paper is only eleven inches long. If you leave an inch on top and bottom, that provides a working length of nine inches. So what? Well, if you are new at writing, and if you have trouble pulling your thoughts together, you may find that the very act of inserting a fresh page into the typewriter is an obstacle. Perhaps this is an obstacle faced only by those who use a typewriter, but it is real enough.

I have a vivid memory of my first major writing effort—a thesis. I can't believe how difficult it was. Not only was my hold on the content minimal, I didn't know how to write in the stylized language of academe. I bled for every word, excruciated for every syllable. It was so difficult that if I had to change the paper in the middle of a sentence I often lost the sense of what I was writing. The short paper obstacle. My solution was to go to the local radio station to borrow some teletype paper. That type of paper is just one long sheet fan-folded into a box (like computer paper). I put the paper on the floor behind the typewriter, fed it into the machine and eliminated the need to change paper. Another obstacle removed. (I still feel pity for my poor professor, who was occasionally faced with the task of reviewing four or five feet of ragged prose.)

Another way around the short paper obstacle, of course, is to use a word processor. With a word processor your words scroll up into limbo and you keep on typing. (I don't use one for early drafts, partly because I haven't figured out a way to get it to reward me for writing. On the other hand, a word processor can keep you from stopping at the end of each page or losing your train of thought in the middle of a sentence.)

Many writers would (I'm sure) snicker at calling short paper an obstacle to writing. But then, you will, too, after you have written enough to get the hang of it. The important part is not to stop the flow until you *do* get the hang of it.

Visible words

The very words you have written can be an obstacle. After all, they are right there on the page, obviously in need of revision. You can begin to stare at what you have written and begin musing about how you really ought to rewrite it. You can mentally push words around, and then begin thinking about changes that need to be made elsewhere. Yes, those recently written words can be a real trap.

The way out of this one is to remind yourself of the "first you get it down and then you get it good" rule. Tell yourself that you won't revise what you have just written until you reach the end of the page. Nobody is going to see it in its present shape, anyhow.

If you want to go back and make revisions on the spot, by all means go ahead and do so. Just don't *stare* at what you have just written and tangle yourself up in *thoughts* of revision. Either fix it or move on.

Here again the word processor offers a mixed blessing. On the one hand most of what you have written scrolls up and out of sight (making it more difficult to worry about revising what you have just written than when your just-written pages sit beside you). On the other, the word processor makes it so easy to fix your mistakes that you may have a tendency to sit there tinkering with one paragraph. That's just fine when it's tinker-time, but it's a real obstacle when it's getting-it-down time. I get around this obstacle by typing the first draft on a typewriter and then, when the cutting and pasting gets me close to polishing time, I do that on the word processor.

Mechanics

It is very easy to get bogged down in the mechanics of writing. Grammar and syntax can be a problem for those who majored in something other than English or Journalism. You can mix up your tenses, dangle participles, change voices, split infinitives, and commit any number of heinous grammatical crimes. This can cause you to spend a great deal of time fixing, rearranging, looking up— just plain fussing.

But the name of the game is to communicate, not to be grammatical. *If* the rules of grammar can help you communicate, fine! But they are no good as an end in themselves. And if you are being taught by someone who knows grammar, but who doesn't write, you'll be taught to write until you are grammatical; you won't be taught to write until you communicate.

Don't get me wrong. If you can't write a coherent sentence at least once in a while, you're not likely to turn on any editors, let alone communicate with your readers. But you don't have to be able to recite the rules of grammar, and you certainly don't have to be able to follow all those rules. Heck, that's what editors are for.

All you need to be able to do is say what you want to say, and then go back and fix it so that it says what you want it to say in the mind of the reader. That's easier said than done, of course, but not by much. Here's what to do when you aren't sure of the grammar or syntax (I'm not even sure what syntax is, but I know you've got to have some). First, when you have trouble with the structure of a sentence [*That's syntax. Ed.*], either write something, no matter how poorly constructed it may be, or let it dangle. Second, begin the next sentence with, "In other words, . . ." and complete the sentence. Third, make a mark in the margin to remind yourself that you will return *later* to tidy up. Know what you'll discover? You'll discover that most of the time the sentence that began with "In other words" is the one that says it best. All you need do then is to delete the first sentence and remove "In other words."

In any case, you can save the grammar fixing for later drafts. First get it down, and *then* make the repairs.

Sequencing

An exasperating obstacle can be that of sequencing, or flow. It is possible to find yourself all tangled up and stopped simply because what you are writing doesn't seem to go smoothly from here to there. The problem can be with the flow of chapters, or it can be with the flow of ideas within a chapter, or even with the flow of sentences within a paragraph. Even if you have an outline, you can find sequencing a troublesome obstacle. After all, the existence of an outline doesn't mean that the flow depicted by the outline is a useful one to the reader, and an outline doesn't help with the flow of a paragraph.

But! (Fanfare) There are ways to skewer this obstacle with a mighty lunge, and the two skewers are called Standback and Getitdown. Each is thrown into the breech when one of two sequencing enemies attacks.

The first of these enemies is one that might pop up while you are expanding a note, explaining a concept, or even while you are writing merrily along. "Wait a minute," it says. "This doesn't belong here. It doesn't *flow* from what comes before." And then it sneaks up and whispers with a loud shout, "And *you* don't know where it belongs!"

Oh, woe is you.

So you sit and stare. But what has happened is that your mind began to think of two things at the same time. You were doing nicely in explaining something, when all of a sudden your mind took a leap to the larger picture and "saw" that what you were writing ought to go somewhere else. It may not be able to tell you *where* it ought to go at that moment, it may only tell you that something is out of place. The remedy is to reach for Standback. Stand back and remind yourself of what you are trying to do *at this moment*. Say to yourself, "Now look. Right now I am trying to complete this paragraph (section, chapter). When I get through with that, *then* I will think about where it should be moved." And say, "By the time I have finished what I am doing, I will probably know where it should go." Draw a circle around the puzzling piece and then get on with what you were doing.

The second sequencing enemy might strike when you are puzzling about the outline (sequence). You may be stuck because you simply aren't sure where things should go, or even which things should be included. When that happens, reach for good ole Getitdown. Tell yourself, "I don't have to think about sequence *until* I have something to sequence. So first I'm going to get it down, and then I'm going to put things into a useful flow."

If you will use the ploys I've just described, the obstacles to getting it down shrink to the point where they will be smaller than your power to deal with them.

Smoothing It Out

Yesterday my wife came into my office (hers is next door) and the conversation went something like this:

She *What's wrong?*
Me *What do you mean?*
She *You're just standing there, looking glassy-eyed.*
Me *I'm sort of floundering around. I just finished the first draft, and I don't know what to do.*
She *That's weird.*
Me *I know it, but I feel like Wile E. Coyote when he runs off the end of a cliff with his legs still spinning, knowing that the big drop is about to come.*
She *So let's celebrate. How about starting with a hug?*

When you've been working hard, and regularly, on a project, and when the project is suddenly over or you reach a big milestone, there is likely to be a letdown. There is likely to be a period when you feel washed out, lethargic, or just plain lost. That shouldn't be a surprise. It often is, just the same.

But that letdown may not be a letdown at all. It may be just plain fatigue. After all, writing is hard work and it takes a lot out of you, even though it doesn't involve a lot of physical effort. And since the completion of a first draft is a form of ending, a form of closure, it's a natural place for the mind to want to take a break. Unfortunately, it is also a place where self-doubts may begin to creep up on you. Who am I to write this thing? Who would want to read it? Maybe it's no good. (I know them all by heart.) But if you know a letdown may be on its way, you can meet it head-on, and counterattack.

Completing the first draft, no matter how tentatively, is a major milestone, a major victory, and therefore a major reason for rejoicing. So put the manuscript away and come up for air. With a great deal of deliberation, do the following:

1. Tell yourself that it is natural to have a letdown and to think cloudy thoughts when a first draft is finished.
2. Tell yourself that you are fully aware that your book still needs work, but that you have finished a draft and the hardest part is done.
3. Tell yourself that even if you do nothing further you have done a great thing. You have begun, you have persevered, and you have created something that never before existed in the history of the entire world.
4. Tell yourself that you have earned the right to take a few days off from the project and that it is time for celebration. Then reward yourself. While thinking about the pages you have written, do something you really enjoy.

But get away from the project for a while. How long? Maybe a day, a week, a month. That will depend on how long it takes you to feel ready for the next steps.

Shaping it up

I know a man who writes and rewrites every page until he is satisfied with it. Two pages a day is his quota, but when he's done, he's done. (It makes dull reading, but he's done.) He never goes back to completed pages to see if he can make them better, and he doesn't try out his work on even one of the people it is being written for. If you work that way you won't have to take a break between the first and last drafts. You can get right on with publishing.

But if you're more typical, your first draft won't be ready for anyone to see. If your draft looks anything like mine, it may not yet have page numbers, it may not hang together from one end to the other, it may have some bulky sentences that need ironing, and it may contain some drivel that had to be written to get the fingers started. My first drafts need culling, rearranging, rewording, smoothing. If yours are similar, then shaping is the next step. Now that we've gotten it down, we need to get it good.

I'd like to tell you what I have to do to make the draft ready to be seen by someone else, but I have the nagging feeling that you don't have the same problems I do. I have the feeling as I write this that everybody else finds writing a lot easier than I do and that to reveal the things I have to do to complete a manuscript will expose myself for the amateur that I am. I have the sneaking suspicion that you will heap scorn upon me for not being better at this than you are. That's how I feel at this very moment.

How do I handle such a feeling? A lot more easily than in the past, I'm happy to say. I tell myself that nobody has to see what I write until I am satisfied with it, and so I can go ahead and say anything that I want. I also tell myself that if what I write is of no interest to my readers, they will tell me about it during the tryouts, and so I don't have to worry that inappropriate things will slip out. Having told myself those things, I get back to saying what I think I have to say. So let me tell you what I have to do to a draft to make it into something I am willing for someone to see.

Continuity

Only once can I remember writing a first draft that seemed to have all the pieces in proper order from beginning to end. The other drafts all needed some pieces shifted from here to there. The first shaping step, then, requires that I read through the draft while thinking about whether or not the sequence makes sense. At this point I don't care whether or not it makes sense to the reader—the reader will tell me that during the testing (tryout) phase. But before showing it to a reader it has to make *some* kind of sense; it has to have a flow from one idea to another.

Standback and Getitdown were helpful in overcoming sequencing obstacles while I was drafting, but now it is time to look at the flow of the entire piece. It is time to make it flow in a way that makes sense to *me*, so that I can then take steps to make it flow in a way that makes sense to the *reader*. At some point along the way I will have written a one-page summary of what I think I have to say, in narrative form. Generally it starts out with, "Look. What I want to tell you is this." And goes from there. I'll refer back to that page to see whether the draft reflects the flow implied by the summary. No, I still don't have an outline at this point, but now that I have a draft of what I want to say, I am finally in a position to create one. I will read through the draft, outlining as I go. The outline will show me where things are out of order (usually), and it will show me where something is missing.

So I move the pieces around until I think they are in the proper order, and then draft a table of contents to see what it would look like. That little exercise shows me that my chapter titles are all wet and need some thought. But I don't fix those until later, when the content is nailed down.

To test my sequencing I will "tell the book." I will simply stand up and pretend that I am telling someone about the book. I will explain what comes first, and then tell what comes after that. (You think people who talk to themselves are nuts? Never mind. It works.) Sometimes that isn't enough to tell me about a sticky sequencing problem, so I will find LSW (Long-Suffering Wife) and ask her to let me tell the book to her. I refuse to let her *read* it at this point because it is too early to let *anyone* see it, and because I don't want to "waste" her input. So I tell it to her. When her face gets all screwed up into a pretzel, I sense that something is awry (I'm good at reading those subtle hints by now), and I ask for input. Or she may ask a question that will help me to see just what ought to go where, and I run back to my typewriter to make the fix.

Culling

As I have already said, I will write anything that comes to mind if I am having trouble getting the fingers moving. The result is that the first draft may be peppered with such statements as:

- Now if you bums had any sense at all you would pay close attention to what I am going to say.
- Now then, what I am feeling at the moment is a certain need to tell you about. . . .
- At this point I will need to come back and insert an example.
- Oh, crap. This is no way for a grown man to spend his time.

You may perceive a certain lack of literary merit in the above. Never mind. Comments like those have served the purpose of getting me closer to publication time. But at some point they have to be removed, excised, deleted. So another step is to carry out a crapectomy by crossing out all the verbal baggage. That includes any profanity that may have crept in, as well as emotional diatribes and attacks on the readers' ancestry that may have been written during a fit of frustration. After all, a successful book expresses concern for the reader, and maybe even affection. Anything that suggests otherwise should be removed.

During first-drafting I also include a wide assortment of hilarious asides, comments, and anecdotes. Since most of them are also hilariously distracting and unfunny, *they* have to come out, too. But this isn't so easy to do. As I hate to throw out anything that might brighten up a page and cause the reader to smile, crossing out the funnies is done with reluctance. But again, I don't have to worry about making mistakes in this department; the readers who help with the testing will quickly tell me which of my comedic masterpieces should be scrapped.

By the way, did you notice that the last paragraph contained the answer to the question, "Should I avoid the use of humor?" If you've heard you shouldn't use humor because what is funny to one may be offensive to another, rejoice. Though that may be true, you can feel safe about the use of humor as long as you know your work will be "tested" by intended readers before you send it off for publication. So go ahead. If it doesn't work, they'll tell you. (You can then delete it, and try to get away with it in your *next* book.)

Smoothing

At this point it is time to attend to some of those things that make for easy reading. It is time to unsplit some of the infinitives and to make the tenses match up with one another, and to fix paragraphs that begin talking about "you" and end up talking about "we." It's time to take care of loose ends, such as the insertion of charts, drawings, cartoons, quotes, or other missing pieces.

In addition, it's time to chop out the weeds, the words that get in the way without adding anything to the meaning (e.g., *in order to, for the purpose of*). The editor will deal with that, of course, but you want your manuscript to be as good as you can make it before you let anyone else see it.

Finally, it is time to fix the wording so that the eye can run across it without getting snagged on verbal burrs and bumps. The only sure way I know to do that is to read it aloud. Keep a pencil in your hand as you do so and scribble in the changes that will make it read more smoothly. If it doesn't sound smooth to the ear, it won't read smooth to the eye. I have often been asked how I make my stuff "so readable." The answer is simple. First I *write* it to them, and then I *read* it to them, aloud. Only when it's written in a way that the tongue can handle is it ready for someone else to see.

By the way, if your house plants droop, or if you fall asleep while reading your manuscript aloud, you'll know the manuscript needs fixing. Could it be that it's boring because you have said everything you know about the subject, rather than what will be of interest or use to your audience? Could it be that you haven't taken the time to write out a description of your intended audience? Could it be that you take the subject so seriously that you have forgotten your readers are real people who may not find the fine details of your subject nearly as absorbing as you do?

Could it be that the "fog index" of your writing is too high; that is, could it be that your sentences, and/or your words, are too long? Keep the sentences to twenty-five words or less (with occasional exceptions, of course). Keep the words short enough to be understood by your audience, and you will almost always make the content more interesting. You will surely make it easier to read. If you are writing technical material that requires the use of technical words, make sure your reader knows what those words mean before you blend them into your sentences. And keep in mind that just because you are writing technical doesn't mean you have to write pompous and boring. Readers of technical material are people, too. So keep the sentences short, and (as much as possible) use words that everyone will understand. For example, if you say "endeavor" when you mean "try," you're just showing off. So maintain a focus of consciousness that endeavors toward minimization of polysyllabic verbalisms. In other words, keep it simple.

Opening

Not only do you want your words to be easy for your audience to read, you want your pages to *look* easy to read. You don't want the very look of the page to scare them off. What you want is for the text to *appear* to be digestible, and that means presenting it in bites that *look* manageable. So rather than write pages in the form of solid blocks of type, you will want to open them up with paragraphs, short dialogues, subheads, drawings, cartoons, lists, and space. Especially space.

The rule I try to follow is never to have more than two consecutive pages of solid text broken only by paragraphs (this rule wouldn't hold for stories or novels, of course). If there are more than two such pages in a row, I look first to see whether I can add a subhead. Not only do subheads open up the text, they provide additional road signs that tell readers where they are. Next I review the paragraphs to see whether I can make a list of some items that I have described in a paragraph of prose. For example, rather than say that you can open your text by adding subheads, dialogues, lists, drawings, cartoons, and space, I would consider saying it this way:

> *Here are some of the things you can add to open the text and make it look more readable:*

- Subheads
- Dialogues
- Lists
- Drawings
- Cartoons
- Space

That's a lot better than burying a series of items in the tangle of a paragraph.

So take a look through your manuscript to see what you can do to it to make it *look* as readable as you want it to *read*. Here is one of the places that the book designer and the editor will be worth their weight in gold. The editor will spot opportunities for subheads, for example, and the designer will design a page format that will be pleasing to the eye.

Balancing

There's one more thing to do before letting anyone else see your work: check it for balance, for proportion. What's balance? Balance is, well . . . balance. If you are writing a book of ten chapters, and each chapter contains about twenty pages, except for that hundred page chapter there in the middle, it's out of balance. If one topic is considered in far more detail than any others, the book is out of proportion.

You can see how easy it is for that to happen. While you're drafting your pages, your mind is focused on the words and sentences. You are trying hard to make the words say what you want them to say, and you are trying hard to put them in the right order. And when you get to that topic that you *really* know something about, or that's your favorite, it's easy to let the fingers fly. (And it's right to let the fingers fly whenever they feel the urge.)

But ultimately you will need to check your balance, to make sure that the weight you give the topics isn't out of proportion. That doesn't mean putting exactly the same number of pages in each chapter. What it does mean is checking that the level of detail is about the same for all topics, unless there is a good reason to do otherwise. This is also not to say that you should throw out pages just because one or more chapters seem to be considerably longer than the others. Maybe you need to make

two, or even three, chapters out of one long one. Or perhaps you should add some detail to the shorter ones. If you're not sure which way to go, an editor can help.

First presentable draft

When you have completed a draft of your manuscript, when you have made the changes called for when you read it aloud and otherwise shaped it up, and when you have added most or all of the odds and ends, such as graphs or drawings, you will have the first draft that you are willing for someone else to see. It won't be the first draft that you wrote; it will be the first that you are willing to show someone else—the First Presentable Draft.

You will have a First Presentable Draft when:

1. All the pages are readable (the manuscript is at least typed, even though it may include strikeovers and crossed-out sections).
2. There is a title page.
3. There is a table of contents.
4. The pages are numbered.
5. All the significant pieces are there.

Let me explain the last item. As a working rule, you should always assume that nobody, but nobody, has any imagination at all—except you, of course. You should assume that your readers will not be able to *imagine* anything that isn't right there in front of them, that they can't *hear* anything that isn't actually happening, and that they won't be able to *see* something that isn't right there on the page before them. If, when you ask someone to read through your work, you have to say such things as, "You'll just have to imagine that those charts are here on this page," or, "There are going to be some examples added here," or, "Just pretend that each *he* has been changed to *he or she*, you don't yet have a First Presentable Draft.

When you show it to someone, it will be because you want to know what to do to make it better. If it isn't all *there*, you may not find out what you want to know. When it *is* all there, you will be ready to taste the proof of the pudding. You aren't ready to talk to a publisher yet, but you're getting close. So let's go try it out to see how well it flies.

Fail-safe

Up to this point your writing effort has been directed at saying it, getting it down, and then shaping it up. There has been writing, rewriting, smoothing. Finally, it became a First Presentable Draft, one you are willing for someone else to see.

So what else is there? Isn't it ready for the publisher? After all, you've worked your fingers to the bone, and finally it's all there. Or is it? Actually, it isn't ready for the publisher until it does what you want it to do, as well as you can make it do it.

You see, until now you have been writing to please yourself. You have been writing what *you* think should be written, including and excluding material *you* think should be in or out, and you have been sequencing the material the way *you* think makes the most sense. Fine. But, if you want the book to be published, you have to write it so that someone other than yourself will want to read it. You will need to make the adjustments that will make the readers want to buy it, read it, act on it, say good things about it, and recommend it to others. You've come a long way, but now it's time to shape your book to fit the *reader*—the time has come for the tryouts.

How do you conduct tryouts? By using the same procedure used by tailors to find out whether a suit fits, by motion picture studios to test movies (called previews), and by advertisers to test commercial messages. Practically all people who want to make sure that their product does what they want it to do some sort of tryout; many do more than one. (What's that? You want to know how many tryouts I did of the manuscript of *this* book? About five, and more than one person was involved in all but one of them. You'll find the names of these insolent perpetrators at the end of the book.)

For example, though you have written your book in a sequence that makes sense to you, how do you know it will make sense to the reader? Are the words you used those the reader will understand? Are there any words, or examples, that will turn the reader off? Is the level of detail about right? Does it work? That is, does the book have the effect on the reader you want it to have? These are the kinds of questions that will be answered by tryout.

Before I describe the procedures for tryouts, though, I should spend a paragraph or two to help you keep from falling apart or from bristling to death when someone makes a constructive comment about your work.

Accepting criticism

Accepting criticism isn't easy unless you've had some instruction and practice in how to do it. We don't like to be told that we are less than perfect, and nobody likes to be told that his or her baby, er, book, needs some changes. Criticism usually hurts, no matter how tactfully it is put. And it hurts especially when the criticism is directed at something that you've been sweating blood over for the past umpteen weeks. Just imagine how a young mother would feel if she proudly showed her newborn to her friends who said things like:

"Gee, what an ugly kid."
"Looks like his father, who has a nose like Cyrano."
"How'd it get so shriveled?"

I'm sure you would sympathize with a mother who had to endure such abuse. But what about those who are asked to offer suggestions about how you might improve your manuscript to make it better from the reader's point of view? Who are these insensitive clods, anyway, to come along and say things about your book like:

"What does this sentence mean?"
"I had to reread this part several times before I figured out what you meant."
"Why is this here? It doesn't seem relevant to anything."

The nerve! Even a dimwit should have understood it (bristle, bristle). And the old ego gets in the way of *your* understanding that those comments were not aimed at making you feel smaller, but were made to help you improve the fit between the book and the reader.

Because I'm sure that you aren't any more exempt from the laws of nature than the rest of us, I'd like to offer a suggestion or two to help you deal with these feelings when you do *your* tryouts.

First, tell yourself that there is a difference between collecting information and making decisions about that information. Tell yourself there is a difference between reporters and judges, and that while you are doing a tryout you are playing the role of reporter, not judge. You are simply collecting information. Whether you *do* anything about that information is a totally different issue. You might throw it away, or burn it, or throw darts at it. Or you might sift through it to see if there is merit to any of it.

Second, when someone is giving you reactions and suggestions, and you have reminded yourself that you are simply a reporter collecting information, say *to yourself only*:

"After all, I don't have *to listen to this."*
"He doesn't know what he's talking about."
"If she's so smart, why doesn't she write her own *book?"*

Third, probe for more information. If there is something they think needs fixing, ask them how they would fix it. "How would you say it?" is a good question to use. It will result in some free help in improving your manuscript.

Fourth, remind yourself that those making the comments probably haven't had any training and practice in how to give constructive criticism. A few will be naturally tactful, but most may not be able to phrase their comments in a manner that (a) is devoid of emotional overtone, (b) focuses on the issue, and (c) includes suggestions for improvement. They're doing the best they can, and you will simply have to make allowances for the fact that their skill at constructive criticism isn't as strong as their motivation to be of assistance to you.

Fifth, remind yourself that people will not be able to tell the difference between comments aimed at the content and those aimed at how the content is handled. Tell yourself that they will tell you things about *what* should be in your book when they think they are telling you about your *treatment* of what is in your book. Not only that, they will also tell you about how they would have written it, while thinking they are helping you to improve what you have written. In other words, their comments will not be neatly categorized for you, so tell yourself that you will collect them all *now* and sort them *later*.

Sixth, tell yourself that the people who are helping with tryouts are the *only* experts in the world on the subject of how to shape the book to fit them better. Since they are members of your target audience, they are the ones you are trying to inform, entertain, instruct, mystify, or amuse, and so they are the only ones who can tell you how well you are succeeding and how to succeed better. Writers and English teachers can tell you if the writing is "good" in terms of style, grammar, and syntax, but they *cannot* tell you whether the book is having its intended effect on the reader. Only the intended reader can tell you that. So tell yourself that, though your tryout helpers may be a little clumsy in giving constructive criticism painlessly, they are the world's greatest experts on how well the book is working (doing what you want it to do).

Finally, if you still feel bothered or defensive or resentful about the comments that are made, put the comments away in a drawer. After all, you don't have to *do* anything about every comment anyhow. You don't have to do anything about *any* of them if you don't want to—only if you want your book to be useful to your readers. But you don't have to do it today. Besides, you deserve a break; you deserve to reward yourself at this point with a little time off. So put it all away. For how long? You'll know. When your emotions subside to the point where you can think about the comments more objectively, you'll know it's time to get them out and incorporate those that make sense.

But you *must* do at least one tryout to make the book fit the reader, and you *must* do tryouts if you want the criticism to be given to you in *private* before it's published, rather than given in public afterwards. It's your choice. Frankly, I'd much rather

hear the bad news when there is still time for me to do something about it, rather than after the presses have rolled. Wouldn't you?

There are several procedures you might use for tryouts, depending on what you want to find out. Let me show you how by describing the kinds of tryout procedures I use for my own manuscripts.

Preparing the manuscript

Before you head for tryouts you need to prepare a copy of the manuscript. Prepare?

What's to prepare, you may wonder? Don't you just make a copy? No. For one thing, you make sure the title page has a copyright notice on it. No publisher wants to publish material that has a clouded title, and so you need to take whatever steps you can to assure that the material you send to the publisher is *yours* and no one else's. That's a lot easier if you simply send the manuscript to a publisher without first showing it to others. But since you *are* going to show it to others, and since you are going to allow the copy to leave your control (they're going to take it home with them), you need to try to keep the content from being stolen. (When people steal *words*, it's called plagiarism, but it's stealing just the same.)

"You've gotta be kidding," you're probably thinking. Who would be so sneaky as to steal my stuff? Who would *want* to? Good questions. Answer: lots of people. The crazy thing about it is that most people who plagiarize don't even think of it as stealing. In the first place, they don't know anything about the copyright laws, so they don't know what's legal and what isn't. In the second place, many people believe that if they *need* it, they have a *right* to it. They feel that since they "need" it for their next lecture, or for the course materials they give to their students, for example, they have a "right" to copy your material. And they will.

I know you won't believe that until it happens to you. And it can happen even *after* the book is published. Several years ago a friend called me to ask whether I knew that a professor had published one of my books, in Spanish, with his name as author. I told the friend, "No, I didn't know that, but thanks for the tip." I informed the publisher, and the publisher got his legal arm working. They verified that my informant was correct, and notified the university that employed the professor. Result? The professor doesn't work there anymore.

There is a third reason people will begin using your material before it is published. If it's really good, people may think, "Gee, this is just good, common sense. I knew this all along; I just didn't quite know how to say it." And then they will go off and say it your way, either verbally or in print. The better your book is, the more people will want to get their hands on it. That's what you want, of course, but only *after* it's published, not before.

So the first thing to do is to make sure you put the little copyright notice on the title page:

> Copyright © 19____ by ______________________________.
> All rights reserved.

That will serve notice that the material is protected by law. No, you don't actually have to send two copies to the copyright office to get the protection; you need only make it clear that this is your material. The publisher will later do all the legal work needed for domestic and foreign protection of the published version.

The next thing to do is to write something like this on the title page, following the copyright notice:

> *This prepublication draft is not to be copied, quoted, or referenced; the forthcoming publication version will contain significant changes and improvements.*

That will remind people that this isn't your final work. It will remind them that this is a temporary version and that the published version won't be the same.

The third thing to do is to have a stamp made up—mine says "Draft"—and stamp the message on every tenth page or so. That will make it harder for people to treat your draft as though it were published material (you want them to use quotes only from the finished work).

The next thing to do to prepare the manuscript for tryout is to *make it look like a draft.* What in the world for? Because we're doing a tryout to *learn* something. We want people to tell us their reactions and we want them to give us information that will help us decide how to make a better match between the manuscript and the reader. Unfortunately, if you give them nice, clean, typed copy, they won't be as helpful to you as they would with a draft that *looks* like a draft.

Why? Lots of people take as gospel anything they see in print. They believe what they read in the newspapers and they believe what they read in books. "Why would anyone go to the trouble of printing anything that isn't so?" they wonder. "Who am I to believe I can improve on anybody's book?" they feel. And they will tend to withhold comments because they think if there is something they don't understand, it is because there is something wrong with *them*. And why not? That's what they were taught. If the textbooks were unintelligible, or the explanations incomplete, or the lectures irrelevant, it was always the student who got the grade . . . and the blame. After a lifetime of this sort of experience it is little wonder that people tend to think there's something wrong with *themselves* when faced with poor writing.

So make sure your manuscript looks like a draft. If all the words are correctly spelled and the grammar perfect and the typing clean, cross out a word or two here and there and write it back in, in pencil. Make a note or two in the margin. Put a little question mark in the margin here and there, and scribble "Change?" in the margin at a couple of places. If you make it *look* like a draft, your readers will be more likely to believe that the book is being tested rather than that they themselves are being tested.

Finally, prepare for the tryout by typing your instructions to the reader on a piece of paper, and attach that note to the manuscript itself. That will be useful in reminding the reader of just what you want him or her to do with it; it will be a reminder of the type of information you would like to have.

Tryout procedures

There are several things you can do to find out how well your book is achieving its purpose, most of which involve telling people what you would like them to look for while reading the book. As you read the following tryout procedures, keep in mind that not all of them will be appropriate for your own book; keep in mind that you would use only the ones that will tell you what *you* want to know.

Continuity Check

When I have been working hard on smoothing the sentences, I am likely to lose sight of the whole. Can't see the forest for the trees, and all that. Before I try to find out whether the book does what I want it to, therefore, I give it to a trusted friend for a continuity check. I want to know whether it's all there. At this point I don't care if it flies. I just want to know that it has all its parts and that they are approximately in the right place.

So I give it to a trusted friend, one who can make comments without destroying my will to continue. I instruct him thusly: "I'd appreciate it if you'd read through this to see if it's all there. I'm not ready yet to check whether or not it works. I just want to know whether or not from *your* point of view, it has a beginning, a middle, and an end, whether or not the pieces are about in the right place, and whether or not you feel the content is all there."

And my friend will do just that. He may think it stinks, but he won't say that. With his dulcet voice dripping with compassion, he will tell me that there is a chapter that needs to be junked, a couple of others that ought to be switched, some road signs that need to be added, and some content that needs to be added or changed. In short, he tells me what I need to do to the manuscript before it will be ready to show to strangers.

Content Check

The second check is aimed at finding out whether the book does what I want it to do. Though it may be nice to know that the book is successful in meeting some sort of literary standard or form, it is far more important to learn whether the book is accomplishing its purpose. And if not, why not.

In my case that purpose usually is to inform or instruct, so I want to find out whether the manuscript does so.

To do that I will prepare a copy of the manuscript and add a note reminding the reader of the purpose of the tryout, and how the comments should be made. I'll invite the reader to write *directly on* the manuscript rather than to make comments on a separate sheet of paper. It's a lot easier to write comments on the manuscript itself; nonfunctional words can be crossed out and better ones added directly, and short marginal comments are easier to write than full sentences on a separate piece of paper.

If the purpose of the book is to instruct, I will ask people either to answer the questions included at the end of the book (if there are any), or to answer some questions I attach to the note. If the purpose is to inform, I will ask for comments on what were remembered as the main points.

If your intent is to amuse, mystify, or entertain, your note would remind the reader that you will want to know if those purposes were accomplished, how well they were accomplished, and where the reader sees opportunities for improvement. Finally, tell your readers that all aspects of the book are open to comment and that you will welcome anything they have to offer.

Having prepared the manuscript for tryout, find someone who represents the target audience. (At this point I still try to find a member of the target audience who is a friend. I don't want strangers to see it until I know that it is working.) Tell your tester what you are doing and why, and ask politely whether he or she would be willing to help you out. People like to have their advice sought, so tell them you need their advice. You're telling the truth, after all. Then let them have the manuscript. As you do that, ask them to give you their own estimate of when they might get it back to you. Don't say, "I'll give you a week to read it." They are doing you a large favor by helping you to improve your work, and you should expect to give them a reasonable amount of time to read through it. You are imposing on these nice people who have a lot of other things to do, and you should be as considerate of them as possible. Invite the person to call you by phone if there are any questions.

Then just sit back and sweat it out. Suffer the anguish of not knowing whether it will fly or fall, of not knowing whether it will be considered as having any socially redeeming features, or whether it will be laughed at or applauded. And as you sweat, remind yourself that:

1. "I want to know what's wrong with it *before* it's published, not after."
2. "I don't *have* to use any of the comments I receive."
3. "I'm not alone."

How Many Times?

At this point it would be wasteful to try your work on more than one person at a time, because your first tryout will reveal enough opportunities for improvement that you'll want to make the changes right then and there—before anyone else sees it. For example, if something is pointed out that is just plain wrong, or misspelled, or awkward, you wouldn't need to have the same comments from ten more people before deciding to fix it. Or if you discover that the book doesn't do what you want it to, and you now know *why*, again there is no reason to try it out on more people before making a fix. Not only no reason to, you'd be embarrassed to. So one person is plenty for the first tryout.

How many people do you give it to, one person at a time? As many as it takes to get the book to do what you want it to. Sometimes that means one, but usually it will mean three or four.

After you know it's working, you may want to try it out on a small sample of strangers who represent the target audience. They have less at stake than friends, and are more like the people who will see the published work. Where do you find strangers for this sort of thing? You could advertise in your local newspaper, I suppose. It might even be fun to draft such an advertisement.

> *Soon-to-be-famous author will accept comments about terrific new book.*

My own strategy is to ask my friends to give the manuscript to one of *their* friends, along with the typed paragraph or so of instructions. They are usually glad to do it, and they *know* that their names will appear in the finished book as having helped.

Which is a rule of book writing that you must never, ever break. What rule? Say something nice about each and every person who had anything to do with the creation of your book. Do it in person, or by letter or phone, at the time the service was given, and then later on in print. Keep a careful list of names, and take the trouble to make sure you have spelled each of them correctly.

Attitude Check

Wimps and idiots couldn't possibly be expected to understand what comes next.

That stopped you, didn't it? You weren't expecting to read words like those, and you probably bristled some. And if there were any more of that sort of thing, or if you thought I was serious, you would turn against me, put this volume down, and

never get to the end. You would be "turı
withdraw, disconnect, from these pages. (
secret. The "wimps and idiots" you read abov
version of what I had in earlier drafts. I wanteu to make the point that you can accidentally use words that will turn people off, but the words I started with turned them off so hard, even before I got to the attitude check, that I had to change them to something less repulsive. And then even *those* turned out to stimulate too strong a reaction. See why an attitude check is so important?)

What a waste that would be. After all the work I put in writing something, I want people to *read* it. I want them to read from cover to cover. Don't you?

Unfortunately, one consequence of not being able to read minds is not knowing with any precision just what kinds of words or thoughts will turn the reader off. I know *some* of the things that will cause them to put the book down, but I don't know all of them. I *do* know that if I inadvertently have too many turnoffs in my pages, the reader will go away—and my purpose will not be accomplished. I know that if I put obstacles in the way of the reader some, if not all, of those readers will stumble and quit.

To avoid that undesirable event, I carry out an attitude check on my manuscripts. You can, too. It isn't difficult. Simply give a copy of the manuscript to a member of the audience for which it is intended, along with these instructions:

> *As you read through the manuscript, please make a* mark *on anything that slows you down, turns you off, or rubs you the wrong way. Don't write words that explain your feelings; just make a mark on the words or sections that bother you. If I don't understand the reason for a mark, I'll ask you to explain it. Also, please make a mark on the page you are reading if you put the book down for any reason.*

By asking them to make marks instead of writing words, you will make it easier for them to identify things that bother them. If they have to *explain* it, they may not mention it.

Why ask them to make a mark to let you know where they put the book down to do something else? Because those marks may provide clues to things that need to be fixed. You see, if they put the book down to go to the refrigerator, or to water the lawn, or to count their socks, they may be exhibiting avoidance behavior toward the book. They may be trying to get away from something they have read. They may be reacting to something they interpreted as unpleasant. Or they may find sock counting a more interesting activity than manuscript reading. And I want to know what the problem might be. Of course, people don't count their socks only when they read something that turns them off—but *sometimes* they do. Think about the things you have read. Have you ever put a book down in the middle of a chapter? Why? Probably because you reached a part that was dull, or wordy, or difficult. Or maybe because it was unpleasant or insulting. (Come back here!)

Let me give you a few examples of the sorts of things I uncover during the attitude check. As I told you earlier, I will do anything I can think of to keep my fingers moving. I will insert a flip comment here, and an aside there. This doesn't worry me because I know that I am going to delete them later. And I do. But sometimes I forget one, and sometimes I leave one in that *I* think is just great, but that leaves the reader cold. During the attitude check, the readers will spot these for me, and out those comments go.

Sometimes I will use an example that hits too close to where the reader lives. When I was working on a book intended to help teachers avoid doing things that might teach kids to *hate* a subject while they were learning *about* it, I used an example from a school in a southern state. It was a true story about a group of teachers who were proud of their school because it was integrated. Black and white kids both attended the same school, but many of the black kids had either spotty attendance records, or dropped out altogether. And the teachers made the usual comments, such as, "What can you expect from *those* kinds of people." What they had failed to notice, however, was that the black kids had to leave school for a few weeks during the fall to pick cotton. And when they returned to school, they were "behind" in their work. The teachers also failed to notice that they didn't do much to help the farm kids to catch up, and so it wasn't at all surprising that those kids tended to drop out—from frustration, confusion, or shame.

This example was an excellent illustration of how it is possible to teach kids *about* a subject and at the same time drive them *away* from the subject, and from learning itself. But it had to come out of the book. The readers couldn't face the reality of it. It turned them off so badly that they stopped reading right there. So I had to make a decision. Did I want to kick the readers in the gut with something I thought was "for their own good," or did I want them to finish the book? Obviously the latter, and so the example was replaced with a less emotion-arousing one.

Here are some of the comments that may be triggered by an attitude check.

"I made a mark there because I found it insulting."

"This example is a non sequitur. It just doesn't follow."

"You *may find this funny but I was a little put off by it."*

"I made a couple of marks where you made your point but then kept on beating it to death."

"At this point I flipped ahead to see how long this chapter was going to be."

If readers are confused about something, that is an obstacle and it should be fixed. If they are offended, or made to feel uneasy *with no intended purpose*, that should be fixed as well. Since you are trying to get people to listen to what you have to say, you will want to clear the road of as many barriers as you can. The attitude check helps to identify those barriers so that you can then decide what to do about them.

During tryout of this chapter, two or three people raised this point: "Wait a minute. I can see your point about not wanting to turn readers off, but there are times when the reader simply has to be exposed to emotion-arousing material. For one thing, the purpose of a novel is often to arouse emotions in the reader. For another, readers of medical and homicide texts simply have to be exposed to material that may make them squirm or that may actually cause some revulsion. If they are going to finish the novel or learn the material in the text they will have to put up with their reactions."

This was a good point, and one that is absolutely true. I recall reading a book on homicide investigation whose book jacket consisted of a close-up photo of a hairy chest with a bullet hole in the middle of it. Not a pretty sight, but a lot prettier than some of the gruesome photos I found inside. And the photos barely matched the gruesomeness of some of the cases described in the book.

The issue, though, is one of deliberation. Novelists *deliberately* try to cause their readers to chew their fingernails to the knuckles, and they *deliberately* try to make their readers' hearts pound, or to make them cry or feel hatred for the villain. That's very different from turning off their readers by accident or because of some unintended blunder. Authors of some books (such as the homicide text) often have to include material that may offend the reader. But those reactions are made to content *necessarily* included in the book. They are not reactions to goofs and blunders made accidentally by an author who didn't take the time or make the effort to delete them.

Readability Check

Nobody has to tell you that words can be an obstacle to understanding or enjoying. If I use bigger or more obscure words than I need, I *reduce the size of my readership* by the number of those who don't happen to speak my language. If you don't believe that words can get in the way of understanding, read any government document. Or a doctoral dissertation. Or a legal document. Or a computer manual. It's not a question of looking for the lowest common denominator, or of deleting all special or technical terms. It's a question of removing words that get in the way of understanding.

To locate words that may unnecessarily get in the way of understanding (and therefore words that are reducing the size of my audience), I will sometimes go to my local Rent-a-Kid and rent a pair of twelve-year-olds (usually from a neighbor). I'll give each a manuscript and this instruction:

> *I would appreciate your looking through this book and drawing a circle around any word you don't know yet. It doesn't matter whether you understand what the book is about. It would help me to make the book better, though, if you would circle the words you don't happen to know yet.*

And do they ever! Those rotten kids will draw circles around dozens of perfectly respectable words that have nothing whatever wrong with them except that they can easily be replaced by words that *everyone* knows. (Kids have no respect!) By a rough count I find that at least a third of the circled words can be replaced by words understood by almost everyone. Some can't be replaced, or won't be replaced, because they are technical or special purpose words, words that are needed to communicate the sense of the ideas, words I happen to like a lot, or words that I have made up. There are many reasons for leaving some words as they are, but I'd rather have the potentially troublesome ones pointed out so that I can make a conscious decision to keep them or replace them.

"But I'm not writing my book for twelve-year-olds," you may be shouting. Neither am I. But those kids are helpful in calling attention to words I should think twice about. As I have said, I leave many of them alone. But when circles show up around a word like *elucidate*, I trade it in for *explain*, unless I'm writing for an audience that reveres bulky writing.

This "poor man's" readability check is another inexpensive way of reducing the obstacles between content and reader, and is worth doing. It can be a little hard on the ego, but I'd rather have mine battered *before* publication. Wouldn't you?

Cover Check

After all that hard work on the inside of a book, why would you want it packaged in a brown paper bag? Or in a cover that nobody noticed, or in one that turned them off? If the inside of the book warrants testing, why not the outside? After all, that's what people see first. If *that* turns them away, if you can't even get them to open it up, you haven't any chance at all of accomplishing your purpose. You can't inform or teach them, you can't entertain them—you can't impact them in *any* way.

So, it's worth testing the cover design. Oh sure, it's true that most books are not bought from a rack at the airport, and it's true that the decision to buy your book may not be influenced by the cover. On the other hand, try this little test. Can you think up a cover design that would be so ugly or so repulsive that *nobody* would want to pick up the book it covers? Go ahead, try it.

How about a cover with a picture of squashed eels? Or of a carcass being torn apart by buzzards? Or . . . . If you thought of one, you have proved that there are cover designs that *can* turn people off. The point is, there is a continuum of attractiveness, ranging from attractive to repulsive, and I'd rather the cover represented something on the plus side. Wouldn't you?

But hold on a minute. If this is your first book, and if it's being published by a publisher, you aren't going to be given anything whatever to say about cover design. You just write the words; the art department gins up the covers. Then why describe the procedure for cover testing? Two reasons, the first of which I've already explained. The cover can make a difference in the attitude or expectations with which the reader steps inside. The second is that if it works out that you are going to publish the book yourself, you'll be *certain* to want to test possible cover designs. Since you will want to do everything you can to tip the book in the direction of success, you will want the most compatible cover you can manage.

The procedure is simple. Ask the designer to mock up four to six cover possibilities. If one is black and white, they should all be black and white. If one is in color, they should all be in color. And they should all be the same size.

Take your covers "on the road." Ask anyone you can find (one at a time) to help you make selections. Tell the testers you would like their advice. Then put *two* of the cover designs on a table and ask, "Which of these would you be more likely to pick up?" Don't ask them to explain why—just ask them to pick one up. Put those two covers aside for the moment, and repeat the process with another pair. After the last pair has been presented, present the ones they have already selected, two at a time. Repeat the process until you have the single cover of their choice. Note this winner on a sheet of paper, thank the person for the help, and be sure to spell his or her name right when you write it down for later acknowledgement.

If there is a clear preference among the covers, there is no need to ask the testers for clues about what the problems are and about what might make a cover more attractive to them. Most of the time, however, it isn't that clear-cut, because the designer has come up with several good possibilities. The ones with yukky colors or bizarre designs are easy to discard, but sometimes there is a design that appears to be basically attractive, except for a feature that would be easy to correct.

There's only one thing to be careful about when doing a cover check. Don't ask people which of the pair they *like*. Ask them which one they would be more likely to *pick up*. That way you don't burden them to find a reason for their action, and it will be easier to get their cooperation.

It doesn't take long to do a cover check. A minute or three per person is usually enough. How many people do you try them on? As many as it takes to find out how the designs affect your testers. If *none* of the covers is appealing, you will probably need to test on a dozen people or so before that nontrend becomes clear. At the other extreme, if there is a clear preference for one design, the trend will become clear by the time you've tested on half-a-dozen people. But at only two to three minutes per person we're talking about a small investment of time for a very important activity.

Again, you're not going to have any say in the cover design unless you are established, working with an innovative publisher, or publish yourself. That isn't all bad, since publishers are up to date on current trends and are experienced in the intricacies of cover design.

Title Check

Titles are a different matter entirely. There are probably dozens or even hundreds of cover designs that might work equally well, but that isn't true of titles. Titles use words, and only a small collection of words would be useful in a title. Unfortunately, a word can have different meanings for different people. A word can evoke favorable images in some people and unfavorable images in others.

If you think you know what your title should be before you begin writing, lucky you. If there is only one title that is the obvious choice, or that would be appropriate, again, lucky you. But be careful. The "obvious" choice may not be so obvious to the reader. I once wrote a book intended to show teachers how to influence students to like learning more rather than less. The "obvious" title was "Influencing Attitude Toward Learning." It was obvious because that's exactly what the book was about. But when I tried out the title along with a few other possibilities, using the same procedure as for a cover check, *this* title didn't fly. Worse, it generated some emotional response in some of the testers.

What could be wrong with a title that accurately describes the substance of a book? In this case it was the word "influence." Most of the teachers who tried out the titles simply couldn't bear the thought that they might be influencing somebody. You might wonder what they thought they were getting paid for, but that was beside the point. The title turned them off, but good.

The title that was most acceptable was, "Developing Attitude Toward Learning." It wasn't as accurate in describing the content, but it didn't turn off potential readers before they looked inside. And that's important. So even though you think you've got a sure winner of a title, take a little time to check it out. Make sure it doesn't have a word in it that drives the reader in another direction.

How do you select a title? Hmm, that's not an easy one to answer. You want the title to say what the book is about, of course, and you want it to catch the eye. Beyond that it's hard to say. Sometimes a short title is best, followed by a longer subtitle that better describes the content. Other times a longer title would be the way to go. How to know which to use when? There isn't any rule to follow, but there is a way to get it right. Jot down as many possibilities as you can think of, and ask someone who knows about the project to add a few more (a spouse, perhaps?). Cross off the awkward ones, and cross off the ones that don't really tell anything about what the book is about. Then do a tryout with the ones you have left. If the tryout doesn't result in a clear-cut choice, it will certainly provide you with clues about what will and will not work.

The procedure for a title check is the same as for a cover check. Just make sure that each cover mockup has the *same* background (I prefer a plain white background) and that only the title is different on each. Ask your testers, "Which of these two titles would you be more likely to pick up?" and make a note of the final choice. (Don't forget to spell the testers' names right when you write them down for later acknowledgement.)

After all that effort to find a title that communicates your intent, and is acceptable to your readers, your publisher may suggest a slightly different alternative.

What? After I've *tested this title and know it works?*

Mmm, yes, even so. There often is a difference between an acceptable title and a marketable title, one that will be attractive to the majority of readers over the long run. I'll not bother you with the intricacies of the selection of marketable titles (mainly because I've already told you everything I know), except to urge you to pay close attention to your publisher when this subject is mentioned. Your first impulse may be to bristle. O.K., so bristle a little. But then listen carefully. You may hear some wisdom that will result in the doubling of sales, and therefore in the doubling of your royalty check.

Attitude Adjustment

A number of years ago I needed to hire an artist to join our research group, as we needed someone to create the graphic art that we needed in our experiments. Several bright and personable people showed up for interviews, and their portfolios just bulged with examples of truly wonderful art. But when I asked the magic question, the interview generally took a decidedly different tack. It went something like this.

Me *This is a terrific piece of work (pointing to one of the items in the portfolio).*

Cand *Thank you.*

Me *Suppose you had created that piece for one of our experiments, and early tryout showed that it needed some alterations?*

Cand *Some what?*

Me *Some changes. Suppose that it needed a few modifications to make it serve its purpose better. Would you be willing to make them?*

Cand (Bristling) *Sir, there is a professor at Haaarvard and one at Stanford whom I would be willing to have make comments about my work!*

Period. End of discussion. Next candidate. We ultimately found an artist who understood that even art can be modified so that it serves its purpose better.

Though you may have any of a number of reasons for writing a book, one of those reasons is that you want people to read it when you're finished with it. You don't want them to ignore it, or fall asleep while reading it (wake up, there!), or to put it down without finishing it. Instead, you want their interest to be aroused enough when they see it that they pick it up, and you want them to be motivated to read it from beginning to end (unless you're writing a reference work).

The tryout procedures I've described in this chapter will help you to accomplish that result. And once you've done *that*, you'll be ready to publish. But if, as you read this chapter, you felt uneasy or resentful about the notion of fixing your work on the basis of other people's comments, you may have a little attitude adjusting to do. There are two things that might help. First, remind yourself of all the different people who test their work before going public: producers of plays, producers of movies, manufacturers of products, etc. They do it for a good reason; shouldn't you?

Second, keep asking yourself, "What do I want this book to do?" and then remind yourself that the only people who can tell you whether it does what you want it to are the readers.

When your tryouts have shown that you've gone about as far as you can go, it's time to publish.

Getting It Published

This chapter deals with a topic that doesn't have anything to do with getting your book written. Actually, it wouldn't even exist if it hadn't been for the "demands" of early testers. "You're not done yet," they said. "You haven't told us what to do with it once we get it written." They were right. I hadn't, because I only wanted to write something that would help others to get started and to stay with it until completion. And since I've learned to listen to what the reader has to say, I complied.

So now the chapter exists, but you should skip over it unless you are interested *at this moment* in reading about the steps of getting your manuscript published. If you're ready to start writing, though, go do it. Now. You can read the remaining chapters when you've written your book, or when you're goofing off along the way.

Snaring a publisher

What are the odds of having your manuscript accepted for publication? I dunno. You can read all sorts of statistics on the subject. But in this case the statistics don't count. What counts is what you do to stack the odds in your favor. Maybe it won't be published even then, but *you can influence the probability* of getting it published by attending to the following steps.

Step One

How do you get a book published? First you write a book.

That may sound simplistic or condescending, but I am assured by editors that it is an extremely potent piece of advice. It's true that publishers will sometimes sign a contract on the basis of an outline, and sometimes they will even pay an advance on royalty for just the barest wisp of an idea. But they don't do that for me, and they won't do it for you. That's a situation reserved for the superstars of this world. You and I need to have a product, or at least a partial product, in hand.

But it's to your own benefit to have a book, or at least a few chapters of a book, in hand before approaching a publisher. For one thing, it tells publishers that they won't have to rely on your promise to deliver the goods. For another, it *shows* them what the book is about; they don't have to rely on a description of what it *will* be about. For a third, it will show them that it would be easier to turn your already existing manuscript into a book than one that hasn't been written yet, even by a better-known author. Bird in the hand, and all that. Perhaps most important from your point of view is that a completed manuscript tells the publisher they'd better take a look at it soon, or you'll take it elsewhere. That is, a finished manuscript gives you a little more clout than does an outline. It improves the odds in your favor.

So finish the book before heading for a publisher.

Step Two

Now it's time to select the publishers to whom you will send or take your manuscript. (*Note:* The following applies only to nonfiction. If you are writing a novel, you can't get published without an agent—large cities list them in the Yellow Pages. So do not go directly to a publisher with a novel.) There will be several that publish the type of book you are writing, and you will want to send it to those publishers rather than to others.

How do you find out which are appropriate? Easy. Go to your public library and ask the librarian to help you find a list of publishers. Explain why you're asking, and you'll be helped to find just what you need.

Caution: *Do not,* I repeat, *do not* read or thumb through any writers' magazines while at the library. Those periodicals are written for professional writers, regardless of claims to the contrary, and will intimidate you right down to your shoes. You don't need that, so stay away from them.

Once you know which publishers deal with the type of book you have in hand, decide which you will try first. Call each of the publishers and ask for the editorial department. If possible, talk with the chief editor in charge of your type of book. Tell that person that you have a book about ________________ and then ask how you should submit it and to *whom*. (Don't tell this person *all* about your book. Editors prefer to have it in writing.) It's very important that you have a name to address your letter and manuscript to, since it may get better attention than if you just mail it to "Editor." If you are told that they don't need or want another book on your subject, you have been saved the six to twelve weeks it would have taken for them to tell you that had you mailed them your manuscript cold.

Another worthwhile approach is to consult your friends and acquaintances. Do they know a person at the publisher(s) you are considering? If so, would it be all right to mention your friend's name in your cover letter? Anything you can do to keep from addressing your manuscript to "Occupant" will be worth the trouble. Contacts help the odds.

Step Three

Prepare your cover letter. Your manuscript is dead without one. Read what one editor said in reply to the question, "What do you do when you get a manuscript in the mail?"

> *Well, I open it and read the cover letter, if there is one. If there isn't one, I generally send the manuscript back. Then I read the table of contents and the introduction. I glance at the middle, flip through some pages, and read the end. I never read the whole thing, so everything has to be geared to keeping me going. It needs to look as though it will be easy to work on and easy to publish.*

That should convince you of the importance of the cover letter. What should the cover letter contain? It should

- Tell something about who you are.
- Convince the editor you know something about your field or topic.
- Briefly explain why your book is different from, better than, more timely, or more needed than those already available. In other words, try to answer the question, "Why should we publish this book?"
- Describe the audience for whom you have written your book; if you know how large that audience is and have a figure to quote, it will get attention.
- Include your name and address.
- Be less than a page in length and typed.

And if you have done any testing of your manuscript, be sure to say so in your letter. One editor told me, "I never got a cover letter that said the manuscript was tested. I would have been hellishly impressed had it happened."

Editors can tell you stories about cover letters they have received that you wouldn't believe, or that would have you laughing out loud. For example, here's one that editors say they get once a week. It says, in effect, "I know everything there is to know about ____________________. If you will send a list of topics you would like to have me write about and a contract, I will send you the books." The polite reply says something like, "First you write and then we talk."

But that's mild compared to the letter covering a manuscript about the Mohole. (A Mohole is a hole bored through the earth's crust for geologic research.) It said, "I insist that this book be published immediately, because if we don't stop drilling we will puncture the core of the earth and the earth will collapse."

So make sure your cover letter sounds sane and intelligent. But whatever it says, be sure you type and send one.

Step Four

Check your manuscript to be sure it is in shape to be sent to a publisher. At the very least, it should look easy to work with. That means

1. It should be typed, double spaced.
2. The pages should be numbered. The manuscript should not be in a binder, but the pages should be numbered.
3. It should be *all there*: cover page, table of contents, etc. Drawings and/or diagrams should be as finished as you can make them, even though the art department will do the polishing. Scribbled artwork turns editors off.
4. It should *not* be the only copy in your possession. *Never* let the only copy of anything out of your possession. It might get lost in the mail or in the editor's in-box, or it might accidentally be used to wrap a fish.
5. The title page should have a copyright notice typed on it.

Some time ago my publisher sent me a "manuscript" that had been sent in by an author who had previously published several books. I was asked to look at it because I was familiar with the field and could offer advice on its merit. When I removed the rubber bands from around the pile of papers, I found that that's just what it was—a pile of papers. There was no title, no title page, no table of contents, no coherence from one end to the other. Apparently this well-known person was used to sending his publisher a collection of notes and materials expecting the editor to make it into a book. And some publishers will do exactly that, but not for you or me. I had to report that I couldn't review the book because I couldn't find a book to review. The other reviewers said the same thing, and the "manuscript" was rejected.

If you've followed the procedures described in the previous chapters, your manuscript will look so much better than most that are submitted that it will be bound to get a fair reading.

Step Five

Mail a copy of the manuscript (with cover letter) to three or four likely prospects. You can send it by registered mail if it will make you feel better, but it isn't necessary. If you are worried that someone will steal your book, send yourself a copy by registered mail and then don't open it. That will serve as evidence of ownership if that issue should ever arise. Then wait.

How long? Four to six weeks should be enough. If you don't hear from the publishers in that time, send another letter and ask when you can expect a reply. And send another copy of the manuscript to another publisher.

Why won't you get an immediate reply? A number of reasons. First, it will take time for someone to get to it. It will sit on someone's desk for a period of time before that person even decides who should deal with it. When it finally does get to the right person, it might sit in that in-box for a bit as well. Finally it will be scanned by an editor. If it doesn't fit the publisher's need, it will be returned to you. If it looks interesting or appropriate, on the other hand, it might be sent to one or more outside reviewers for comments. In a way, the more time that elapses without your hearing anything, the better chance that the manuscript is being seriously considered for publication. I wouldn't stake my life on that being true, but publishers don't send manuscripts out for review unless they think there's a good chance they want to publish it. And outside reviewers are s–l–o–w.

But hold on a minute, because the main point is yet to come. Sure, publishers reject a lot of manuscripts for many reasons.

Sure they take time to have manuscripts reviewed. Sure they are more expert than you or I at grammar, style, and syntax. BUT. And this is a BIG but. If writers didn't submit their manuscripts, the publishers would be out of business!

If this is your first book, of *course* you are apprehensive about sending your work to a publisher; the thought of rejection isn't easy to repress. But whenever you feel hesitant about putting your tested work in the mail, remind yourself of these two facts:

1. Some publisher *needs* that manuscript.
2. *You* are not the best one to judge whether your book is publishable.

So go ahead; send it in.

The contract

Should the publisher decide to accept your manuscript for publication (hooray!) you will be sent a contract. At this point you have arrived. You aren't "published" yet, as many things must happen between the signing of the contract and publication. But you will have good reason to believe that your words will be seen in print.

The contract is a legal looking and sounding document, but the meaning is clear: "We, the publisher, own the whole world and everything in it, but in return for all rights to your book, we will give you a pittance." You may think that sounds like author bias, but wait until you read the contract's fine print. And I suggest that you *do* read every word of it before you sign. If this is your first publishing contract, you may be so flattered you won't be able to see the print from the fantasies. Read it anyhow.

Just because the contract is printed doesn't mean you have to agree with all the clauses. After all, a contract is simply a description of what two parties have agreed to. Since the contract was printed by the publisher it describes the terms that the publisher is willing to agree to. If you had drafted it, the contract would look considerably different. If you don't agree with something, you will need to take action. The best thing to do is to collect all your questions and then call the publisher to discuss the issues. This discussion will usually resolve the issues, but sometimes not. Sometimes publishers will simply take the position that whatever they write into the contract is the way it is—take it or leave it. Others may be perfectly willing for you to make the changes you feel necessary or appropriate.

For example, there should be something in the contract that describes the terms under which ownership of the copyright will revert to you. You may not be thinking about that since the book hasn't even been published as yet, but you should. What if the publisher signs you up and then decides not to publish? Do you get the book back? How soon? Under what conditions? And suppose that after the book has been selling for a few years, sales go down to a very low level? At what sales level will the copyright be returned to you so that you could reprint the book if you wanted to? Will you have to pay for the return of the copyright? If the answers to these questions aren't clearly spelled out, you will want to raise them before you sign.

If the publisher can't live with your changes, they may come back to you with a comment such as, "This is a *standard* contract." The implication is that, if it's a standard contract, you should automatically agree to all its terms. Don't stand for that sort of pressure. You're not going to get much in the way of concession if you're unknown, but even so, you should absolutely not agree to terms you feel you cannot live up to.

The contract my publisher used in the past listed the millions of rights he expected, such as the right to decide on the book size and type, the advertising, the foreign and domestic prices, and on and on. And because it was his "standard" contract, it even wanted all opera and musical comedy rights to the work. But I didn't stand for that. I struck out the part about operas and musical comedies. I retain those rights for *myself*. Oh, I knew perfectly well that the stuff I write will never appear in those forms, but it amused me to fantasize a fat opera star singing one of my fables, or a chorus line dancing one of my chapters. It was no great concession for the publisher to let me delete those clauses, so we played the charade.

Me *I, sir,* demand *that these clauses be stricken from this contract. Forthwith!*

Pub (Cringing) *Well . . . all right. You drive a hard bargain, but all right.*

Some years ago I was told a story attributed to Hopalong Cassidy, a movie cowboy hero of bygone days. I was told that when he signed movie contracts he had the foresight to retain the rights to distribute his movies by any means not yet invented. That was no skin off the nose of the movie producers at the time. But it meant that as time went by Hopalong owned all the rights to television, videotape, videodisc, and computer distribution of his works. Not bad! Publishers have since caught on to this loophole and have slammed it shut with the addition of a clause that gives them the rights to things not yet invented.

If you are working with a small publisher, you can expect some flexibility in contract terms. For one thing, smallness means that you will more likely be talking with either the second-in-command or the owner. For another, they won't have so many authors in their "stable" (you'll have to get used to the fact that publishers think of their authors as workhorses) that you will get lost in the shuffle. Large publishers, on the other hand, are different. Because of their size (and multiple layers of management), you should expect considerably more rigidity in contract negotiation (they want you to sign, not negotiate). In addition, you will have considerably less to say about how the book is handled after you *have* signed. They don't want you to tell them how it should be designed, for example, and they certainly don't want your suggestions regarding the cover. That isn't all bad, though, as authors don't know nearly as much about what's good for their book as they think they do.

When deletions or additions are then initialed, the contract is signed, hands are shaken, and, if you happen to live nearby, you celebrate with lunch. Lunch is a very important weapon in the publisher's arsenal. "Take an author to lunch" is the motto. With a lavish lunch the publisher can (a) give you a feeling of real importance, (b) find out how well you will endure the cascade of editorial changes you are about to be showered with, and (c) begin to get you thinking about the next book you will write. The lunch also makes it possible for you to inject little one-up gems into your conversations. "I was having lunch with my publisher the other day, don't 'cha know" or "Do you know what my publisher wants me to do *now*?" Lunch thus generates good will and helps make the author feel important.

Royalties

What about royalties, you ask? Right. What about them? There is little to tell you about them except to say that royalties are influenced by the economy, the timeliness and quality of the work, by policy and custom, by how well the author is known, and by what the publishers think they can get away with. I am told that royalties range from five to twenty percent, with the average toward the lower end of that range—which isn't too bad for unproven authors, once you think about all that the publisher has to contribute in the way of effort and cash to make a book out of your manuscript. You just *write* the *manuscript*; the publisher takes all the risk associated with making it into a *publishable book* and with *getting it sold.* The publisher is the only one who stands to lose—at least financially—if the book bombs. Since the one who takes the largest risk is entitled to the largest share of the profits—and losses—the publisher gets the bigger slice of the money pie.

What if it's rejected?

There are a number of reasons a manuscript might be rejected that have nothing whatever to do with the quality of work. Here are some of them.

- The book isn't suitable for the publisher; it isn't what they do, (e.g., a novel sent to a publisher of technical books, or vice versa).
- The book isn't timely (e.g., they don't need another book on Watergate).
- The book doesn't match the publisher's style or policy (e.g., you write 50-page books and the publisher wants 500-page books).
- The book has no page numbers; it's not easily readable; it's not all there.
- There is no cover letter.
- The cover letter was typed on a dirty typewriter.
- The cover letter was inarticulate, didn't explain why the book should be published (i.e., the letter had no "sell").
- No return address was included (more common than you might think).

Then again, the manuscript might be rejected because it is only half-written, or because it is only a set of lecture notes, or a reworked doctor's thesis, or a semi-fleshed out course outline. Then again, it might be rejected because they have just contracted for a book on your topic, or because they have an author whose feelings they don't want to hurt if they *do* buy a book on your topic, or because the editor who happened to review your manuscript didn't understand its importance or appreciate its potential. There are lots of reasons for rejecting a manuscript. Only a few of them have anything whatever to do with the quality of your writing.

Rejection letters

If the publisher can't or won't publish your masterpiece, you will get your manuscript back in due course, probably accompanied by a polite note or letter. No matter what the reason for the rejection, the letter will probably say that your book doesn't conform to the publisher's needs at this moment. Don't be disappointed that you don't get a long critique of what needs to be done to the work to make it acceptable. After all, the publisher is under no obligation to teach you to write.

But as the old saw goes, one swallow does not make a drink. Similarly, one rejection ought not to make for a winter of despair. As you have seen, turndowns can occur for several reasons, most of which have nothing to do with the quality of your work. So forge ahead. Send it to another publisher, and another. If nobody wants it at all, tell yourself that those publishers don't recognize a good thing when they see it, and keep on writing.

A friend of mine wrote what I consider to be a perfectly engrossing and lovely science fiction novel. He wrote it, and then rewrote it to incorporate the results of his tryouts, and then sent it off for publication. It was turned down. He sent it off again. Only to be turned down again. Eventually he collected a dozen rejection notes, and then quit writing. He has a lot of talent and a charming style when he writes. But he quit writing. Just because some publishers didn't accept his first attempt. How sad.

Would it be possible to turn the receipt of rejection slips into a positive force? Knowing that writing is a craft that has to be learned through practice, how about considering each turndown as putting you one step closer to the day when your work will be accepted? Might be worth a try. If you get enough of them, you can write a book about rejection letters.

Do it yourself

There is another way to diminish the effect of rejection letters. Actually, the ploy is also useful for helping you over some other hurdles, such as the self-doubts that can creep in when you think about all those high-powered people at the publishing houses pawing over your work.

Publish it yourself!

No, you don't actually have to *do* it to take advantage of this ploy, you have only to threaten to do it. Whenever you worry about whether a publisher will accept your book, or fume about the changes they might insist on, or come up with some other imagined hassle, tell yourself, "These are problems up with which I will not put. I'll just go right ahead and publish it myself." Go ahead and say that aloud once. There. Didn't that feel good?

Once you think about it, though, you may realize that the idea of publishing yourself isn't as far-fetched as it used to be. Oh, it involves some work, of course, but self-publication is well within the realm of possibility. After arranging to generate two double-spaced, typed copies of the manuscript, you rent an editor to edit (*never* publish anything without having it edited), and a designer to design it (more about book design later).

Once the book is designed, edited, and the title and cover designs tested, you're ready to think about going to press. You get bids from three or four printers, decide on the quantity you want to print, and find somewhere to warehouse the "product." Then you decide how you're going to market the book (nobody will buy it if you don't advertise it), and start writing the ad copy. . . .

Mmm. Come to think of it, doing your own publishing can be a royal pain. You have to do a lot of things you'd rather not do, that you aren't any good at doing, and that you don't want to become good at doing. But then, maybe you'd enjoy the things a small publisher does and it might suit you just fine. If you want to explore the possibility further, now is the time to head for the library to look at some of the writers' magazines. You'll find all kinds of information that might help, and you'll find that lots of people actually do their own publishing.

Perhaps you've noticed that I did my own publishing of *this* book. I didn't want to. After all, I had a "standard" contract from a large well-known publisher, and everything looked like money in the bank. But one day, while talking with the acquisitions editor (the one assigned to review in-coming manuscripts), I detected a strange note. And further discussion confirmed it. This editor wanted to control the content of the book (sometimes referred to as censorship). In particular, she wanted to make sure that the last two chapters reflected the views of the publisher rather than those of the writer. She wanted those chapters to reflect the policies of *her* publishing house, and she wanted me to pretend that those are *standard* policies followed by *all* publishing houses, which is not true.

So, rather than sign myself into an unacceptable situation, I decided to publish it myself—knowing full well that I'd have to do a lot of things I'd rather not do (such as write advertising).

There are other reasons you may decide to do it yourself. You may, for example, feel very tentative about the content and want to be able to pull it off the market if the reactions don't suit you. (When a book is selling, the publisher sells it, regardless of how embarrassed the author may be about it.) Or you may want to take a fling at the direct-mail business. That can be very lucrative, and maybe your book is a good product to start with.

But your first book ought to be published by a real publisher. They know what they're doing, and they will handle details of printing, warehousing, billing, distribution, and on and on. Besides, if you publish yourself you won't have any opportunities to spice up your conversations with little gems like, "I was talking to my publisher the other day and . . . ."

Making a Book

"It's already been a *week* since I signed the contract, and it hasn't been published *yet*! What's *taking* them so long?"

After all that work, after finally finishing the project, you want to see it in print—*now*! You've done your part. Why aren't the publishing people doing theirs?

Oh, do I know that feeling. I may have taken months, or even years to finish a manuscript, but when I have finished it, I want to see it in print right away. You may feel that way too, and when you don't hear anything for a few weeks you may wonder whether the publisher has secretly decided to scrap the project. Why does it take so long?

Because a manuscript is not a book. A *manuscript* is a collection of typed sheets of paper. A *book* is a bound collection of pages whose content is coherent and relatively consistent. Turning one into the other requires a good deal of work by a number of people. Some of it by you. And that takes time. How much time? Anywhere from six to eighteen months. Oh, it's true that a publisher can publish a book almost overnight, but that treatment is reserved for those hot books that are politically timely. Usually, a fast publisher will take about six to eight months to publish.

Though this book isn't about publishing, it might give you a feel for the flow of things if I briefly describe the process for producing a book. As an author, though, you probably will be personally involved only with editing, galley proofing, and marketing. But a glimpse at what happens between these steps may help you understand what's *taking* them so long.

> *Caution:* If you are ready to write your book, put down this book and go do it! If you are not interested in the process of making a book *at this moment*, skip this chapter. You can come back to it later.

This chapter is included, however, because the process of making a book out of your manuscript is part of writing the book—your input will be needed during the editorial steps, and beyond.

Editing

The first step is that of editing your manuscript. The publisher will assign an editor to the project and will try to select one who may know something of the subject and who will work well with you. After reading through the manuscript the editor may call you on the phone to get to know you a little, and to develop a feel for your style, your intent, and your way of working. Once this rapport is established, the editor will get to work on the manuscript in earnest over the next several weeks.

There is much to do. Even though you've worked hard on your manuscript, and even though you have honed and polished, polished and honed, there will be any number of issues to resolve. Does this chart warrant a whole page or can we reduce it to half a page? Should this section be replaced with one describing a different example? We need at least four more subheadings in this chapter. Participles have to be undangled, tenses made consistent, and sentences clarified. And on and on.

In fact, when the edited manuscript is returned for your approval or comment, there will be so many "flags" (notes from the editor) pasted to the margins of your pages that you should prepare yourself for editorial shock. Don't be insulted by the changes, though. After all, when you were writing you were concentrating on the ideas rather than on the details of grammar, syntax, and style consistency. And even though you may have worked very hard to make sure that your ideas are clearly expressed and your structure sound, the editor may have questions or suggestions that will improve upon what you have. So you should expect that there will be flags and marks on the manuscript.

The job of the editor is to make the book publishable. That means making it coherent, readable, and economical. Sometimes that means doing nothing more than ensuring grammatical consistency. In that case only a few changes are in order, and work goes quickly and gives the author little or no pain. Sometimes it means rewriting entire paragraphs and/or moving sections from here to there. And though it is not the job of editors to tamper with your meaning, or with your style, they will sometimes do that unintentionally. That means you will have to fight back, demand justice, rant, rave, and turn blue until the "good

The "flag" is the low-tech medium of communication used by editors to badger authors into submission.

stuff" has been returned unharmed. In other words, it is appropriate to "negotiate" the sticky items. For example, here's a typical "negotiation" dialogue that I have had with an editor.

Ed *What's this word?*
Me *That's* peripheralia.
Ed *I see that. What does it mean?*
Me *What do you think it means?*
Ed *Things on the edges of the main thing?*
Me *Of course. You can tell what it means by looking at it.*
Ed *You can't use it.*
Me *Why not?*
Ed *It's not in the dictionary.*
Me *So what?*
Ed *You can't just go around making up words.*
Me *Why not? Lots of people make up words, and then they get* put *into the dictionary. After all, dictionary writers are followers, not leaders. They go around picking up the verbal droppings of humanity and put them in alphabetical order.*
Ed *People won't know what it means.*
Me *Aha! I've* tested *it on readers and they* do *know what it means. Besides, they say they like it and to leave it in. Tell you what I'll do. I'll give you two split infinitives and a bulky paragraph in return for this word.*
Ed *Oh, good grief.*

You can tell by the smooth, suave manner in which I handle these interactions that the editor is always persuaded by the good sense of my position. (And, as they say, if you believe that, I have a bridge to sell you.) The point is, there will be changes that you should be eager for the editor to make, and there may be some you should fight to prevent the editor from making.

Only once was I assigned an editor who insisted on changing the meaning of my sentences, over and over again, apparently because of some unusually strong biases. Her most blatant pretzel-thinking was saved for my fable, which I had created to highlight a key point of a book.

In this particular book the fable was about a turkey who went out to shoot himself some Troubles. But in the sentence, "A long time later he burst upon a naked Trouble splashing in a pond," the editor had crossed out the word "naked" so hard that she actually made a hole in the paper.

Why? Well, it turned out that she had a bizarre bucket of worms in her head that told her naked means nasty. Not only that, her biases caused her to change my intended meaning in at least two dozen other places. Instead of making *my* book better by editing it, she tried to turn it into *her* book by changing it. Definitely *not* what proper editors are supposed to do.

But that episode was extreme. All the other editors I've worked with made dozens of very positive contributions to the quality of the book. They made it smoother, more readable, and more consistent. Even though they are often rather rigid about what is "proper," they are indispensable. [*Yes, we are. Ed.*]

So when you receive the edited manuscript and see all the flags, try not to panic. In the first place, some of the flags will only be questions about things needing clarification. In the second place, most of the changes will be of the sort you will agree with. Just remember that a manuscript is not yet a publishable book, and that the job of the editor is to make your book, and therefore you, look as good as possible. Third, if your editor is or was an English teacher, some of the flags may even offer some praise for a sentence or three, and an occasional "Good!" or "Well done" is certainly welcome.

Rather than thinking of flags as indications of problems, therefore, think of them as the editor's way to engage in dialogue with the author (that's you). So read through the comments, make the changes, and then talk with the editor about any questions you may have. And here's the best part: good editors are willing to negotiate. If you have strong feelings about one or more of the changes, chances are the editor can find another way to make it work to your satisfaction.

By the way, someone other than your editor usually will do what is known as the copy edit. This is a final check for grammar, syntax, and style consistency that is done after the editor has

Book Design

While you are dancing with the editor about this or that, the book designer is doing his or her thing—de-signing the book. What does that mean? Somebody has to decide how large the pages will be, what kind of type and leading (space between lines) will be used, and where the page numbers will go. Somebody has to decide whether paragraphs will be indented, and where the chapter title will appear on the page. And somebody has to make sure that all the design elements fit the nature of the book and that they don't clash with one another. In other words, somebody with an artist's eye needs to come up with a list of specifications that will tell the ~~printer~~ typesetter and printer how to turn the manuscript into a book.

Designers are the people who will make a book look stylish or dull. They ~~'re the people who will give it a classy look, provided they are kept under control. Designers are artsy-type people who~~ can make it look so attractive that people will have to pick it up. They can give it that classy look, that just fits the classy content. Or they may see your book as an opportunity to apply some far out, off-the wall ideas. ~~They may, for example, try to~~ maybe specifying a typeface that is trendy, but inappropriate for your book. Mostly, though, designers will do great things for your work. You may never get a chance to work with the designer, but a good editor can pass on the necessary information to the designer so that the design fits — and enhances — the content.

165

AM 13

Above: Manuscript page as decimated . . . ah . . . edited . . . by editor.
Opposite: printed version of the same page.

completed her (you are as likely to run into a male editor as a male nurse) work and before the manuscript is set in type. It is a good idea to try to get your publisher to agree to your checking the manuscript after the copy edit, just to make sure that nothing important has been changed. Usually all will be well, but it is always a good idea to check. Sometimes a copy editor will make style changes so that it no longer sounds like you, and you will want a chance to fix any little problem before it becomes permanent (published).

Book design

While you are dancing with the editor about this or that, the book designer is doing his or her thing—designing the book. What does that mean? Somebody has to decide how large the pages will be, what kind of type and leading (space between lines) will be used, and where the page numbers will go. Somebody has to decide whether paragraphs will be indented, and where the chapter title will appear on the page. And somebody has to make sure that all the design elements fit the nature of the book and that they don't clash with one another. In other words, somebody with an artist's eye needs to come up with a list of specifications that will tell the typesetter and printer how to turn the manuscript into a book.

Designers are the people who will make a book look stylish or dull. They can make it look so attractive that people will have to pick it up. They can give it that classy look that just fits the classy content, or they may see your book as an opportunity to apply some far out, off-the-wall ideas, maybe specifying a typeface that is trendy, but inappropriate for your book. Mostly, though, designers will do great things for your work. You may never get a chance to work with the designer, but a good editor can pass on the necessary information to the designer so that the design fits—and even enhances—the content.

Galleys

Once you and the editor have agreed on wording, the manuscript will be set into type. Ahh, finally. But not so fast. There are still a few steps to complete before the presses roll.

The text will be set into type, all right, but when a proof is run it will look like one page a mile long. This will be sliced like salami into strips usually about two feet long, and each strip, called a galley, will be numbered. The object of this step is to make sure the typesetter didn't make any booboos. So somebody

Galleys are proofread, corrected, and sliced like salami into pages.

has to check to see that the type was set according to the specifications established by the designer, and to make sure all the typos are caught for correction. That somebody is the proofreader.

Sometimes typesetters will use the wrong kind of type for headings or subheadings, and sometimes they will forget to use boldface when called for. I've even had a typesetter who used a different *size* of type for italics; fortunately, it was caught in time and reset.

There will always be some typos—words misspelled, words left out, lines repeated, and so on. Those have to be corrected if you want a good-looking book that doesn't put the reader off. If you are given a chance to proofread the galleys (and you can negotiate that privilege during contract signing), do it with diligence. Look at them carefully and mark everything that doesn't look right. You don't have to know the proofreaders' secret code for marking; just mark it the best way you can. The editor can make the right marks on the copy that goes back to the typesetter for correction. And be sure to have someone else proofread it as well. Even though the publisher has someone proofread the galleys, no single person ever catches all the goofs—the more eyes that scan the copy the better. Warning: this is *not* the place to make changes or to start rewriting the book. The publisher will charge you for editorial changes after the book is set into type, other than the correction of typos, and rightly so. It's very expensive to make changes at this late date.

Dummying

If the structure of the book is relatively complicated, the next step will be to make up a dummy. This simply means that a mockup of the book will be made by slicing up a copy of the galleys into pages and then pasting these onto book-size sheets of heavy paper. The finished dummy will let everyone see just what the finished book will look like. Well, at least they will be able to see what goes on which page.

Somewhere along the line you may be asked to adjust your prose to fit the design of the book. *What?* Mangle my words to make the *design* come out right? Mmm, yes. Suppose the design calls for each chapter to end on the left page, and there are a couple of chapters that would do that very nicely except that there are about two lines left over. The intellectual discussion with the editor goes something like this.

Ed *We need to shorten this page by three lines.*
You What? *But we just worked our tails off to get it to read right.*
Ed *We need to shorten this page by three lines.*
You (On your knees, doing Hamlet) *But that's the* best part. *You'll completely destroy the meaning. Why, do you realize how long it took me to* write *that page?* (Wipe eyes with hanky)
Ed (Ignoring the tantrum) *If we deleted this sentence here, and these five words there, it would fit nicely.*
You *Are you* serious? (Flailing arms and stamping foot) *I don't know how I'll survive if you take that out.*
Ed *Well then, which lines do* you *think we can cut?*
You *Arrrgh! You sly dog. You did it to me again.*
Ed *I'll give you 'til sundown to make up your mind.*

Paste up

Many books will not involve paging problems and so a dummy is not needed. That being the case, the next step is for the typesetter to make the corrections discovered during the proofreading of the galleys. Having done that, the typesetter will send the designer "repro," a clean, camera-ready, what-you-see-is-what-you-get copy of the manuscript. This is the version that will eventually be photographed by the printer. This step is almost never shared with the author.

This copy is then pasted onto boards, page by page. A "board" is literally a piece of cardboard ("chipboard" in the cardboard biz), and there are as many of them made up as there are pairs of left and right pages.

The boards are carefully checked to make sure that the pages are pasted right side up and in the right order, that all the corrections have been made, and that there are no smudges or broken letters (kinky type) or other things that shouldn't appear on the printed page. This last look is important because this is the camera-ready material that goes to the printer, and because every change from this point on becomes very expensive. It is highly unlikely that you will be asked to check the boards.

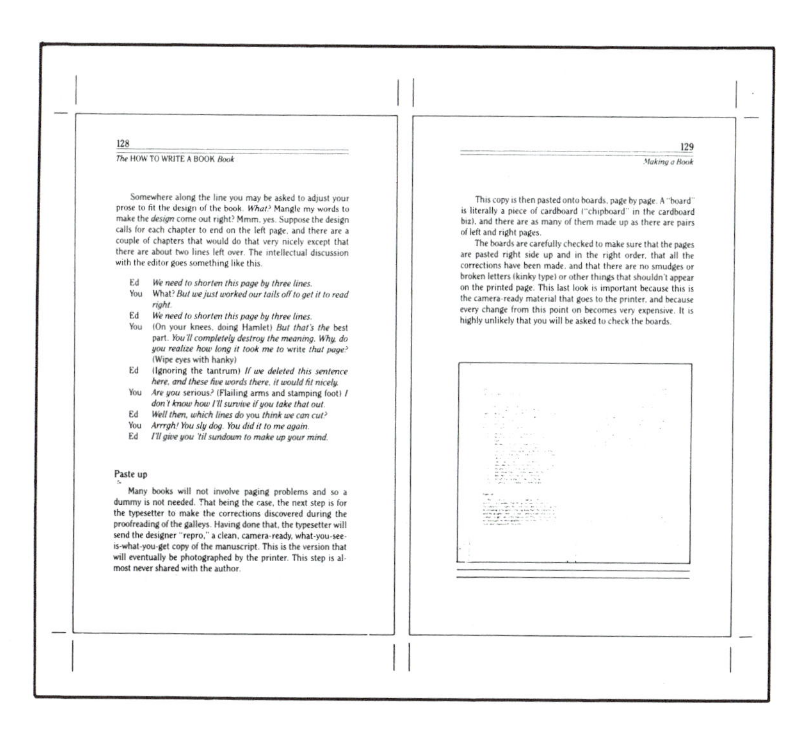

128

The HOW TO WRITE A BOOK *Book*

Somewhere along the line you may be asked to adjust your prose to fit the design of the book. *What?* Mangle my words to make the *design* come out right? Mmm, yes. Suppose the design calls for each chapter to end on the left page, and there are a couple of chapters that would do that very nicely except that there are about two lines left over. The intellectual discussion with the editor goes something like this.

Ed *We need to shorten this page by three lines.*
You What? *But we just worked our tails off to get it to read right.*
Ed *We need to shorten this page by three lines.*
You (On your knees, doing Hamlet) *But that's the* best part. *You'll completely destroy the meaning. Why, do you realize how long it took me to write that page?* (Wipe eyes with hanky)
Ed (Ignoring the tantrum) *If we deleted this sentence here, and these five words there, it would fit nicely.*
You *Are you* serious? (Flailing arms and stamping foot) *I don't know how I'll survive if you take that out.*
Ed *Well then, which lines do you think we can cut?*
You *Arrrgh! You sly dog. You did it to me again.*
Ed *I'll give you 'til sundown to make up your mind.*

Paste up

Many books will not involve paging problems and so a dummy is not needed. That being the case, the next step is for the typesetter to make the corrections discovered during the proofreading of the galleys. Having done that, the typesetter will send the designer "repro," a clean, camera-ready, what-you-see-is-what-you-get copy of the manuscript. This is the version that will eventually be photographed by the printer. This step is almost never shared with the author.

129

Making a Book

This copy is then pasted onto boards, page by page. A "board" is literally a piece of cardboard ("chipboard" in the cardboard biz), and there are as many of them made up as there are pairs of left and right pages.

The boards are carefully checked to make sure that the pages are pasted right side up and in the right order, that all the corrections have been made, and that there are no smudges or broken letters (kinky type) or other things that shouldn't appear on the printed page. This last look is important because this is the camera-ready material that goes to the printer, and because every change from this point on becomes very expensive. It is highly unlikely that you will be asked to check the boards.

A matched pair of verso (left) and recto (right) pages.

Bluelines

The printer now photographs each of the boards to make the film that will go onto the presses. To make sure the film is clean (free of pinholes and other blemishes) and sharp, the printer will run off a proof to be checked by the editor. This time the proof is called a "blueline," and is likely to smell of ammonia. This is because the proof is run off on a white print machine, so-called because it is also used for making blueprints. I'm sure you will see the logic of that better than I.

Marketing

While typesetting, pasting-upping, and proofing are going on, somebody in the publisher's organization is thinking about how to sell the finished product. Will it be advertised in magazines? On television? At the meat counter of the grocery store? Hawked on street-corners? Will a brochure be prepared? Whom will it be sent to? (Naturally I wrote "Who" in that sentence, but the editor had to butt in again.) [*Butt of course! It was a compromise—it could have become "To whom will it be sent?" Ed.*]

You are likely to be asked to help out with this process. No, you won't be asked to write the advertisement (don't even ask), but you may be asked to provide information about

- Yourself (so the marketers will know what kind of superlatives they can get away with)
- Who the intended audience is (so they can decide where to aim their advertising)
- What journals, magazines, newspapers, or other periodicals are read by the target audience (to provide clues about where to advertise)
- Names and addresses of people to whom the publisher should send complimentary copies (to help spread the word about this terrific book)
- Names of book reviewers who would likely review the book favorably

You are not likely to be given a chance to review and comment on draft ads, even if your contract says you will have that right. Marketers will kill to prevent authors from having anything to say about their marketing schemes and materials. If an ad contains blatant lies or other embarrassing material, you can and should make a lot of noise to the publisher, of course; but it is unlikely you will get a chance to check the ads before they're published. Even if the publisher wanted you to do so, the tight deadlines would make it very difficult.

Publication!

At last the day has come. The book is out! You will receive the number of copies called for by your contract and, if you're lucky and live nearby, the publisher will take you to lunch. As you leaf through the pages, you can savor the thought of a job well done. It may not be the best book ever written, nor one that will last forever in the minds of the readers, but it was written, it was completed, and, by golly, it was published! You can be proud of that. It is appropriate to have a "publication party." Invite your friends over for a suitable celebration, and be sure to have your book casually strewn about. A copy framed in neon lights and placed on the mantlepiece is casual enough. In short, rejoice!

Reviews

After the glow of publication wears a bit thin, a gnawing feeling will begin to eat its way toward consciousness. "What will they say about it? Will they like it? Woe is me."

While you were sitting there contemplating your next book, the first one was being *reviewed.* "Aha!" snickered the reviewers, rubbing their hands together. "Here's another book I can tear apart. I can't write 'em myself, of course, but I can sure pick holes in the work of others." That *must* be the way they think. I've had reviews written by people who obviously had never read the book, by people who reviewed it from their *own* point of view rather than from that of the *intended audience*, and by people who compared the work to standards having nothing whatever to do with the purpose of the book. Of *course* it isn't fair. But then, reviewers aren't required to have special skills to write reviews; anybody can do it. They don't have to worry; nobody reviews the reviewers (at least, not yet). It isn't all that bleak, however. You just may luck into one or more reviewers who actually know something about the subject of your book and whose reviews represent an accurate evaluation of the book.

There will be some highly intelligent reviews (favorable, that is), and they are the only ones to save. Learn from the criticisms, but remember that the reviewers are not the readers. Some of them have influence on whether your book will be bought and read, but they are not the readers you were writing for. If you have tested the manuscript with any of the procedures previously described, you will have done all you could to avoid serious criticism. So relax and just let it happen. Sticks 'n stones, and all that.

Autographs

One day when you least expect it, someone will sidle up to you with a copy of your book in hand and ask you to autograph it. What? You're kidding! You want *my* autograph? Aww, shucks. It's going to happen so you'd better think about how you will

handle that situation. Think about it now so that you won't accidentally mishandle it when it happens, either because it catches you off guard or because of embarrassment.

How should you handle the request for an autograph? Handle it gently, compassionately. Remember that the person asking is likely to be somewhat nervous about the request. It may well be the first time in that person's life that he or she has asked anyone for an autograph, and you will not want to hurt any feelings. What should you do? Act flattered (which you should be), sign the book, and then thank the person for asking. You don't have to *say* anything in the book, just write your name and the date. People who ask for your autograph are paying you a large compliment. Treat it as such, even if you feel embarrassed the first few times it happens.

Come to think of it, it's rather nice to be able to go home and say, "You know what m'dear? Three people asked me to autograph a copy of my book today." Mmmm. Yes. That has a nice ring to it.

But for that to happen you have to write a book.

So what are you just sitting there for?

Get it down! Get it down!

The Forever Beacon

"Stop the ship," screamed Bugeye Zzyt.

"Whaddaya mean, stop the ship?" queried Zzilly Twitt.

"Stop the ship!"

"Holy frillipps! We're going thrice the speed of light, and you holler, 'Stop the ship'? Are you having space spasms?"

"I thought I heard a Beacon."

"That's different," said Zzilly Twitt, as he put on the space brakes. After screeching to a stop between two nicely shaped asteroids, they turned on their M1 Beaconsniffer and tuned.

"There it is," screamed Bugeye. "I knew I heard it."

"What is it?" puzzled Zzilly.

"It's a Forever Beacon—that's what it is."

"Never heard of 'em. What're they for?"

"Don't you vacuum suckers learn *anything* at the Academy? A Forever Beacon is what's left of a quaint custom started on Earth. Whenever Earthlings wanted to immortalize someone for something, they would set up a Forever Beacon. It would broadcast their names and deeds throughout space until it dropped from exhaustion a few million years later. Space law says everyone has to stop and listen."

"What's this one for?"

"Wait a minnit. I'll get a read on it," said Bugeye, and proceeded to twiddle the twaddles of his Intergalactic Beaconreader, Model M3. "Aha," he said after a dramatic pause for effect.

"What's with the 'AHA' already," grated Zzilly, impatiently.

"Oh, seems some guy wrote a book and wants everyone to know who helped him with it."

"Wasn't he good enough to do it alone?"

"How should I know? It was written leventy-seven thousand years ago."

"They probably had to have help with everything back then."

"Yeah. You can tell the way it says he *wrote* a book, instead, of saying he *thought* a book. Dead giveaway."

"Uh huh. So what's it say?"

"Can't *you* tell?"

"Sorry. My Beaconspeak isn't nearly good enough. So translate already so we can be on our way."

"Well, he names the people who helped with the various types of tryouts. Seems he kept testing the thing until it did what he wanted it to do."

"Makes sense."

"Says that a David Cram helped with the initial continuity check."

"Hey, didn't we run across that name a few times on some artifacts we dug up on that rundown planet in the Milky Way?"

"Think so. Must'a been a very helpful guy. But there's more. Says that Paul Whitmore checked the psychological accuracy to make sure the content reflected sound principles of motivation management."

"Gory frambitz!"

"It says that A. Robert Taylor graciously provided the REAL WRITER photo, and Joe Harless offered big time moral support at a critical moment.

"Then there were several people who tested for effect to make sure the book did what it was supposed to do: Danny Lyons, Helen Wick, Bill Valen, Jack Vaughn, Judy Springer, and Judy Vantrease Wilson. Says they all worked their way through the manuscript and were kind enough to offer reactions and suggestions."

"They probably didn't have anything else to do in those days."

"And then Brad Mager, Bev Graves, and Eileen Mager gave it an attitude check."

"A what?"

"An attitude check. Seems this author wanted to find out if there were things that rubbed readers the wrong way. Wanted to eliminate the obstacles, he says. And then he says that Ken Mettert, Jill Maxey, Bill Valen, Linda Marsh, Carol Valen, and Eileen Mager helped test the cover designs."

"Cautious soul."

"And lissen to this. He says the editor, a Mary McClellan, kept butting into his prose while fixing up his busted sentences and unsplitting his infinitives."

"The nerve!" expostulated Zzilly. "Anything else?"

"Yeah. Says the project manager, designer, paster-upper, and otherwise all-around bottle-washer was Susan Pinkerton of S & M Productions."

"She whipped it all into shape, is that it?"

"Never mind. Here's the last part. It says we should stand in admiration of all these people. . ."

"Stand? On what? Does this guy think civilized people go around on *legs*, for Zzork's sake?"

"Just a figure of speech. It wants us to respect the contribution of these folks, which was deeply appreciated, and to call the Forever Beacon to the attention of everyone we meet."

"Sounds fair enough. If *they* could put up with this guy. least we can do is spread the word on their behalf."

Which is exactly what they did.